Transcendent Thought and Market Leadership 1.0

How to Lead Any Profession, Anywhere in the World

Bruce Raymond Wright

When you engage Bruce to learn to think and act transcendently, you will find he helps you actuate parts of your brain that are typically underused. I've seen him do this one-on-one and with audiences of thousands of people. In many ways this book is like having a transcendence conversation with Bruce. This book probably won't *feel* like a typical business and leadership development book. It will bounce ideas throughout as much of your psyche as you are willing to allow. The more willing you are to activate underutilized portions of your brain, the greater your results will be. Hang on and enjoy your ride into more transcendent thought and action.

— Steve Matter
Author and retired Fortune 500
Senior Executive at numerous companies

Publishing-Partners
Port Townsend, WA 98368
www.Publishing-Partners.com

10 9 8 7 6 5 4 3 2 1

Printed in the United States of America
Library of Congress Control Number 2016930318

ISBN: 978-0-9862830-9-3
eISBN: 978-1-944887-14-8

Chief Editor: Colleen Walsh Fong
Cover Design: OctagonLab
Cover Image: Leslie Lee
eBook: Marcia Breece

Contents

The Purpose of This Book in Your Business and in Your Life

My deepest intention for this book is to help *you*, and all of the leaders, managers and/or entrepreneurs connected to you, to stretch your imaginations so you begin to see possibilities for greatness that have been invisible or unavailable to you. I invite you, your colleagues, those whom you lead, and your advisors to learn how to think bigger, broader and deeper about evolving into the position of market leader. My wish for you is that you will follow the formula and some of the examples provided here and actually create new standards of excellence in your niche. Or, if you are truly bold enough to be transcendent, you can create a whole new market to lead.

When *you* are the creator of a new elevated vision and standard in your niche and you share it widely and deeply enough, you will have seized the position of thought leader. Throughout history, the most memorable thought leaders have been transcendent. If you choose to take your position as thought leader and ride it to commercial success via a unique process, business construct or product, this book will help you become the market leader in your field.

Market leaders generate more cash/profit and create greater equity value for shareholders than those companies that fail to become or choose not to be the most prominent player or market leader within their niche. The most prominent professionals and companies that lead their markets *attract* customers/clients that lesser players pursue. Market leaders more easily attract investment capital and they attract unsolicited buyers who offer higher prices and better terms on the sale of the enterprise. Being transcendent will earn you market share and respect that ordinary people and average companies do not enjoy.

Use this guide to step into your fullest potential and glory in your profession to manifest *your* greatness, abundance, and significance in business and in your personal life.

Dedication

This book is dedicated to the loving memory of John Edward Tyson (October 29, 1942 – April 25, 2015). When I first met John, he hired me to be his Exit and Entrance advisor and mentor. John recognized the need for an outside perspective that would help him exit the current phase of his life and help him clarify and achieve the best life that he could dare to imagine. I advised John on a vast array of business and financial decisions, but what most people don't know is this; John was the best business leadership mentor with whom I have worked. In many ways this book provides some of the best recipes that John Tyson and I used to accomplish what many claimed was impossible. John and I had a lot of fun helping people break away from popular yet very flawed beliefs. One example is our dismantling of "A rising tide lifts all boats." I share it with you here.

A Rising Tide Does NOT Lift All Boats

When I was a boy, my family kept a small fishing boat and a camping trailer at Lake Casitas. Over the course of a few days a terrific rain storm blew in and it dumped an enormous amount of rain in a short period of time. This resulted in massive flooding at Lake Casitas. The storage lots where the campers and boats were (secured on their own trailers) became submerged and ruined.

A few years later we were studying past Presidents of the

United States of America and eventually we explored the presidency of John F. Kennedy. Of course, like many people my age and older, I can still remember exactly where I was and how the people around me responded to the news of President Kennedy's assassination. The death of John F. Kennedy had a big impact on my life in that moment and well into the future. I find myself missing his candor every time I experience a modern day politician parsing words and putting him or herself (or their love of power) over the needs and best interests of our country.

To this very day the only JFK speech I take issue with is the one in which he declared, "A rising tide lifts all boats." I know for a fact that statement is not true when it comes to boats attached to trailers.

Metaphorically that statement is often untrue when applied to human beings. This is because many human beings are so firmly attached to flawed beliefs and ineffective behaviors and/or so unwilling to be lifted that they are self-determined to sink and lie at the bottom so that no one can lift them. Nothing can lift a person who refuses to align him or herself with effective thinking and then act with appropriate courage, power, tenacity, and discipline.

In my business we have long applied this principle:

> We are dedicated to helping everyone and anyone who is sufficiently willing to elevate him or herself.

Another way of looking at leading human beings is this:

> They say that you can lead a horse to water, but you cannot make him drink. We say this; we only have enough energy to work with horses who are already thirsty enough to be willing to drink.

The wisest and most effective leaders I have ever known possess a deep understanding of how important willingness is for leaders and their followers. It is unwise to invest one's time, talent and resources with those who lack sufficient willingness to elevate themselves.

When George W. Bush announced his "No Child Left Behind" program, I cringed. I thought, "Here we go again" with another delusional politician failing to recognize that with human beings, it is impossible to lift those who resist elevation. Sometimes it is due to flawed parenting, flawed teaching, or flaws within the students. Some of us are born with profound learning challenges or physical limitations that would keep us from operating within average standards.

I invite all leaders to find and apply memes and create programs that empower every sufficiently willing and capable person to elevate into higher effectiveness. I discourage the use of inappropriate absolutes that are easily proven to be false or that disempower those who cannot achieve excellence or even "average" standards, even when they are incredibly dedicated and willing to be elevated. I encourage using honesty and wisdom to empower people to transcend into greater effectiveness. My dear friend John Edward Tyson would have insisted this book contain this message.

Acknowledgments

Without the help and focus of these exceptional people, this book would not have come into form as it is now. They helped me to improve readability, continuity, and enable me to make my thoughts more understandable and impactful. I am deeply grateful to each of them.

This book's Chief Editor, Colleen Walsh Fong

My unconquerable colleague and General Manager, Melinda ("M") Mordue

Artist who painted "The Dilemma," Leslie Lee

Quality Control/Editor, Steven Drozdeck

Psychology Editor, Dr. David Gruder

Technology Alchemist, Matt Wride

Flow Editor, Lorraine Wride

The great love of my life, Jeanine Wright

Introduction

Throughout recorded history most people have known who the most prominent people, companies, or products are — at least within a given region. Second graders know who the toughest kid is. They know who the fastest kid is. Both tend to be proven and widely accepted. Prosperity, fame, influence and power belong to the most prominent leaders in each category of human endeavor, profession, and known market. If you are the three hundred and thirty-fifth most prominent and respected tax lawyer, home remodeler, real estate agent or termite exterminator in Los Angeles County, you might have to also work as a pizza delivery driver to pay your bills. The top two percent of the professionals in many fields tend to earn five to twenty-five times what their lesser known "competitors" earn. Tax lawyers who are also pizza delivery drivers are not very well respected or as profitable as they would like to be. There are no financial, strategic, spiritual or tactical advantages to being beneath the top five percent in any field of endeavor. This book is for bold courageous people who are willing to elevate their thinking and behaviors into alignment with what is necessary to be exceptional, a champion, a master, and/or THE market leader.

Within these pages you will discover some important timeless and well-proven truths pertaining to the thinking, characteristics, and behaviors essential to human excellence, market leadership, and transcendence. Each time you read this book you will be able to gain more insight and perspective if you study it very carefully. Those who skim or read it passively will receive less from it than those who read it as though they were using it as their guide for a course they are teaching on this subject matter. Studying assertively, as though you are intending to teach others, is the key. I wrote this book to help you move beyond common and self-limiting beliefs, behaviors, and habits that so many people allow to separate themselves from personal excellence and market leadership.

The term *transcendence*, used throughout these pages, means surpassing the ordinary and elevating above the status quo with amazing and relevant offerings, products and excellence that is irresistible. Transcendence and change are inextricably connected. Just as people avoid or resist change, they tend to avoid or resist transcendent elevating new ideas, business, political, financial, or societal constructs that stretch beyond the limitations of their comfort zones or the way they see themselves. I am telling you this so you will not be surprised when some (or perhaps all) of the people around you do not share your enthusiasm for elevating yourself or your business above the current condition.

Here is a timeless observation about human nature that has applied to the subjects of change and transcendence for thousands of years:

> Most people are too comfortable with where they are now to do what is necessary to improve their condition. Even when they are miserable, most people will fight to maintain the status quo. This is especially true for those who are paid to support the status quo.

The truth is many people are so comfortable with ordinary or normal levels of professional performance or personal quality of life that they have no desire or plan to rise above mediocrity. Their desire for normalcy exceeds their desire for excellence. People with that state of mind are highly likely to be indifferent or resistant to your desire to stretch the boundaries of excellence in ways that would make you the market leader.

People who are comfortable with or in love with the status quo are probably invested in you remaining within your status quo. So, be forewarned. As soon as you decide to move above and beyond your status quo, they may see you as a threat to their status quos. It is a yin and yang sort of thing. Almost every great idea and new action meets with a significant amount of resistance.

Here is a neat "little" conundrum or paradox...

To become a prominent masterful expert or a company that leads its market, one must have uncommonly high levels of competency, confidence, boldness, tenacity, and courage. This could be misinterpreted as having an uncommonly large ego. However, those with overly large egos or the self-deluded actually have an unusually low probability for achieving market leadership, especially in highly discerning consumer markets. This is because measurable performance plays such a large role in market presence.

The world is full of self-deluded, egotistical people who oversell, over-promise, then under-deliver. You either have the right offering and deliverables or you do not. Self-deluded politicians, professionals and companies tend to prove they are delusional by making claims that cannot withstand a reasonable level of scrutiny. Discerning people scrutinize claims. They perform due diligence and research beyond the depth and breadth of "ordinary" people so they are less likely to be duped by scam artists, corrupt people or institutionally-centered business models. Because of their uncommon levels of due diligence, discerning people tend to avoid many of the problems (and losses) that "average" people suffer.

Those dedicated to becoming and/or sustaining market prominence or leadership are constantly testing and improving their offerings and deliverables. They rely upon more than their own perceptions (wishful thinking and egos) to determine the effectiveness, impact and importance of their offerings. Wise people who insist upon being market leaders obtain unbiased assessment of their visions, business plans, personnel, capital needs, business processes, offerings, deliverables, moral compasses, customer experiences, and viral connectivities with customers. Ego is trumped by actual, measurable realities, especially performance.

To lead your market, you need to transcend false ego, fear, doubt, integrity deficits, and the common thoughts and behaviors that result in mediocrity. Just as importantly, you must be willing to acknowledge who and what is elevating, relevant, and effective from what is not. Then you must separate yourself, your career, and your company from business models, offerings, policies, and people that either cause or perpetuate mediocrity. This might not be easy for you or many of those around you. Some people, especially those who are offended by benchmarks that prove their performance is not up to the standards necessary for prominence or market leadership, may feel offended by or threatened by factual evidence. Please remember that feelings are chosen. Each of us has the power to elevate our feelings and performances. Let this book help you rise above limiting feelings and rise to new heights of excellence.

I have explained and simplified key details in ways to make this as acceptable, easy, and fast for you as possible. Simple and easy are often different constructs. Even in this streamlined form, few will find implementation to be as easy as they would prefer it to be. That, my friend, is where the opportunity for you to elevate and excel will be found. Right there in your ability to transcend the perceptions, feelings, doubts, fears, resistance, and discomfort thresholds which trap so many people and companies.

Back in the mid-1970s, I had a basketball coach who was fond of saying, "There are two kinds of people and teams in this world. Those who move so fast they kick up the dust and all the slow people who eat their dust." Today's technology empowers us to transcend almost any physical limitation such as speed or strength. These days, one person with a computer (perhaps only a smart phone) and the right vision, courage, and tenacity can prove to be fast and strong enough to overtake the biggest global conglomerates. Let the speed and the strength of your mind carry *you* to a higher level of excellence and market leadership. Allow yourself to think and act *transcendently.*

Chapter One

The Convergence of Leadership and Stewardship

Like many firstborn children, parents and adults would tell me that I was responsible for my two younger brothers. They began putting the mantle of stewardship and leadership on me before I was six years old. I don't recall any of them actually teaching me what stewardship or leadership entailed exactly. They spoke in vague terms that I was supposed to somehow interpret in ways that protected or helped my younger brothers.

Like so many leaders and stewards around the world, I received no detailed training from amateurs or professionals. I wasn't given a formula to follow or a crystal clear list of expectations and specifics as to how I could or would achieve the desired (but very unclear) results.

One day when I was approximately ten years of age, my parents told me to take my younger brothers down the street to a neighbor's house to play. As usual I was told they were my responsibility and I needed to "take good care of them." On this particular day, my parents' irresponsible behavior and unrealistic expectations backfired on them. It also nearly landed my stepfather in jail for child abuse.

This event happened about two years after my family moved within California from Santa Monica to Culver City. My best friend from Santa Monica, Fernando Torres, moved

> **"Just as we develop our physical muscles through overcoming opposition — such as lifting weights — we develop our character muscles by overcoming challenges and adversity.** —*Stephen R. Covey*

on to my block in Culver City. Fernando and his family moved into a house that happened to be exactly the same number of houses down the street from me as they had lived in Santa Monica. I now believe this to be synchronicity but all the adults called it coincidence. Whatever you think it is, I was thrilled to have my best friend back in my life.

As my brothers and I were playing in the cul-de-sac with a few neighborhood friends, Fernando's family's moving truck arrived and I offered to help them move into their new home. Fernando's mother agreed to let me help, but she felt it would be dangerous (and probably annoying) to have my little brothers in our way. I knew that if either of my brothers was stepped on or in any way injured, I would be punished, even if I wasn't the one who caused the injury.

Mrs. Torres urged me to take my brothers home then return to help. That all made sense in my ten year old brain. I had forgotten all about how important "adult time" was for my parents. I had forgotten that they would be very angry if they were disturbed. All I could focus on was keeping my brothers safe and helping Fernando move into his new house.

I took my younger brothers home, sat them down in the living room and turned the television on at a low volume. I was careful to be quiet because we had very strict instructions to be absolutely quiet when our parents were in their bedroom with the door closed. Once I was certain that my brothers were clear about being silent, I headed back down

> **"Nature is cruel, but we don't have to be.** — *Temple Grandin*

the street to Fernando's house. I should have realized that young boys are incapable of keeping still for more than a few minutes. So it didn't take long before they had interrupted my parent's secret activities in the bedroom.

A couple of hours later, I headed home for lunch still ecstatic about re-connecting with Fernando. As soon as I walked in the door, both of my parents began yelling at me, calling me irresponsible and disrespectful. I was told I would be given the worst beating of my life. At that moment my step-father grabbed me by one arm and very forcefully dragged me out into the backyard. There he made me stand for several minutes while he carefully selected "just the right" branch from our nectarine tree for my beating.

William F. Wright had given me many spankings and had punched me and kicked me numerous times before, but this type of a beating would be a first. I was more terrified than I had ever been in my life. I stood there crying from the pain in my now injured shoulder, which happened while being dragged into the yard. I was ordered to stop my sniveling or the beating would be even worse.

After what seemed like an eternity of terror, guilt, and shame, I was dragged by my other arm into the bedroom I shared with my two brothers. The beating would occur inside so my screaming would not upset the neighbors. I was told to count out each of the twenty blows, but after the fifth or sixth strike, I could not count any more. I couldn't even scream anymore. My whole family watched this beating so it would serve as a lesson to all. My stepfather warned us that anyone who shirked his responsibility would get the same treatment.

My fragile little body and mind were in shock. I only spoke when ordered to do so for the next couple of days. After a few days, the cuts had scabbed over and I could stand and walk by myself so I was sent to school. Fortunately one of my teachers noticed that I wasn't moving very well. Eventually she kindly and lovingly convinced me to go with her to the nurse's office. Once there, my teacher and the nurse convinced me to lift my shirt. As soon as my teacher saw the scars and scabs on my back and ribs, she began to cry. She couldn't even bear to stay in the room to see what had been done to my butt and legs.

After school that day I went down the street to visit my friend Amy Early. Amy's mother June asked me if I was injured and I couldn't even muster an answer.

June carefully lifted my shirt. She inspected the rest of the damage, looked into my eyes and promised me that I would never suffer such treatment again. A short while later Amy and her father and I went to McDonalds for dinner while June went to my house and confronted my stepfather. With the help of my teacher, my school nurse, June Early, and the police, William F. Wright learned a lesson about stewardship ... and so did I.

Many years later my friend Mark Kastleman and I were returning from a mountain biking/business trip at Lake Tahoe when our topic of conversation turned into a contest about which one of us had the worst stepfather. The verdict: it was determined to be a tie.

Most importantly that conversation wove through many aspects of our lives as fathers, husbands, friends, business-men, leaders, and stewards. Each of us had been severely abused, traumatized, and wounded by our stepfathers, by certain athletic coaches, bullies, and to a lesser extent, by our mothers. In spite of all of the physical, mental, emotional, and spiritual abuse, we somehow had discovered how to let go of the idea that we were victims. Despite all of the psychologists and science that indicated that we would grow up to be abusive alcoholics, we completely abstained from all intoxicants. We had chosen to learn how to think and behave with kindness and equanimity with ourselves and with others. Especially with our wives and children. We studied and devoted ourselves to figuring out how to find positive energy and even valuable lessons and skills (buried somewhere in the abuse). We had each found good examples (outside the family) to emulate. Our inquisitive attitudes and deep study had empowered us to become extraordinary in several critical areas of our lives. At the very least, our stepfathers had been shining examples of what we did *not* want to be. They were excellent examples of ineffective unloving tyrants who misused their power, leadership, and stewardship opportunities with us.

Contemplating my stepfather's (and my mother's) deficiencies as stewards helped me notice, study, compare, and emulate the thinking, attitudes, and behaviors of effective stewards. I suppose I could simplify this as follows:

We get to choose whether we will be Oppressive Tyrants over others or to be Understanding, Compassionate, and Loving Leaders and Stewards with others.

It comes down to choosing whether to be Coercive, Manipulative, and Forceful vs. a being who provides Enlightened Guidance and Leadership into Empowered Highest Self.

I have been a student and practitioner of Enlightened Stewardship and Leadership since the early 1970s. One of my most important revelations was this:

My mind and its deep conviction to timeless principled beliefs serve as stewards over my emotional response to temporary circumstances and sometimes irrational ego and emotionally driven self.

This does not mean that I do not feel tempted to let my emotions rule me. I am a very passionate and emotional being. I am just as tempted to rush to judgment as are other people. I am just as tempted to feel fear, bigotry, anger, and offense as other human beings. However, almost 100% of the time my elevated sense of self-stewardship wins the moment and the day.

The Wisest and Most Effective Leaders and Stewards Possess Equanimity

Equanimity is one of my most beloved ways of being and it is also one of my favorite subjects to teach and mentor. At first equanimity can be a difficult state of mind and way of being to move into alignment with. I soon realized that each time I put myself into that state of being, the more time I wanted to BE and remain there. At times this required more love or patience with self or others than I was used to or comfortable with. The more frequently I arrived there, the easier it was to find my way there. The next time you are tempted to rush to judgment, or to treat others differently than how you want to be treated with compassion, love, and gentleness, find your way into equanimity and you will have achieved a previously unimaginable sense of calm. In such a state, you will be a more effective steward over your less evolved or lower self. And you will be a more attractive, effective, and impactful leader with those around you. Without equanimity you will not achieve your highest self or your optimum potential as a leader, steward, parent, or fiduciary.

"I believe that one defines oneself by reinvention. To not be like your parents. To not be like your friends. To be yourself. To cut yourself out of stone. *—Henry Rollins*

Equanimity comes from Buddhism. It is a way of getting into and being in the flow of knowing when to be quiet and when to speak up; when to be passive and when to be assertive; feeling the right timing and the right speed to create the appropriate flow. I like to think of it in terms of automobiles. Cars have many moving parts and gears. Equanimity is the oil that lubricates everything, allows things to flow freely and without damage.

Effective self-stewardship demands equanimity, self-respect, self-love, gentleness, patience, and enlightened principled behavior when you are most tempted to be ruled by emotions, led by lower self, or by an agitated crowd. The wisest self-stewards I know are consistently (if not constantly) demonstrating enlightened principled behavior over tempting emotions. Wise elevating leaders do <u>not</u> guide people into an absence of equanimity or into fear, prejudgment, bigotry, or victimhood. As an alternative, optimum stewardship and leadership is focused on guiding and supporting others into higher awareness, effectiveness, and desired results.

Power from the Past
Great leaders and stewards help people elevate themselves into higher awareness, hopefulness, faithfulness, personal power, self-discipline, responsibility, courage, and significant positive results. However, there are a lot of people who

obviously prefer leaders that can only lead those who exist in a state of low awareness, fear, victimhood, and anxiety. These are frightened, disempowered, under evolved, undisciplined, or irresponsible people who are not focused on or dedicated to the achievement of tangible, significant and positive results. Leading people in those conditions is exhausting. If you are not mindful and disciplined, their drama tends to become your drama. I refuse to lead or act as a steward for people in those conditions. My sense of stewardship and love for humanity causes me to provide free and low cost ways for them to lead themselves to a higher place where I am inclined to give more of myself. When acting as a leader remember this: some people have mental illness, birth defects, or injuries that are likely to be outside of your training or ability.

Rather than casting people aside when they are not ready for or able to understand or apply what you offer as a leader or steward, you can lovingly point them towards others who have the ability to help them. Plus it is important to remember that neither you nor I are the best person at a given time and place to lead or help EVERYONE. We can only help or guide certain people, not everyone. Lovingly letting go of the idea that everyone should respect, agree with, or apply our leadership or methods is healthy for us personally and for others. This also applies to parenting as you will see later in this book.

Business leadership is optimized when leaders also take on the mantle of stewardship and dedicate themselves to elevating others into their highest and most effective selves. An organization populated with more evolved mature people is more likely to excel. Such an organization is more likely to become the prominent player in its market. Such an entity would tend to be braver, bolder, more innovative, and inclined to attract and retain mature-minded, high performing, balanced people. An organization like that could sustain market prominence indefinitely.

Chapter Two

The Dilemma

Leslie Lee is one of America's most insightful and talented artists. Her work was introduced to me at the end of a four-day retreat where my colleagues and I had been teaching the audience how to imagineer transcendent thought and put it into commercially viable action. One of the retreat participants said something like this to me, "Bruce, I have a friend who has created a painting called 'The Dilemma.' I think you should use it in your courses and retreats. I think it will help people gain a clear picture of their condition more quickly." My response was, "Please send it to me as soon as possible."

About a week later we received a greeting card with an image of "The Dilemma". We were so impressed that we immediately contacted Leslie and acquired a licensing agreement to use that picture as a book cover. At that time I didn't know what the book title would be, but I knew that it would deal with the universal human dilemma we are confronted with in business, finance, spirituality, politics, and life. This is that book and yes, Leslie's picture is that poignant.

For the past decade I have only shown "The Dilemma" to family, friends, and clients. This book is the first time that I have shared it with the world. Please do yourself and those important to you a favor and study "The Dilemma" carefully. Make note of as many details as you can see. At a minimum please consider these details:

- The person's arms are full of ordinary looking eggs that represent the life, business, financial, spiritual, and relationship circumstances the subject currently "owns" or lives with.

- Imagine how disconcerting or frightening it would be to have a large bird suddenly land on your head. Lots of golden opportunities show up in ways that can be frightening or uncomfortable. In this painting, the person is looking up, but all that can be seen is the head and part of the neck of a large goose. The person cannot see all that is happening and is therefore unable to determine that a golden egg sits on top of his or her head.

- It's easy for us to see:

  » There is a golden egg (not an ordinary egg) resting on top of this persons' head.

  » The goose that laid that egg is about to leave the scene right now.

- The person doesn't have sufficient clarity to know for sure that letting go of some of the ordinary eggs to grab the golden egg, or the goose, will leave the subject better off. The risk is obvious; the reward is not clear nor is it certain.

- Neither you nor I as third party observers can be certain that what the subject must let go of will turn out to be worth the sacrifi e.

- The person is only certain of this: reaching up to grab what is new will end some current aspects of his or her life.

"The Dilemma" by Leslie Lee

The Undistorted Mirror

When facing such a dilemma it would be nice to have a quality mirror with good lighting so we could see what is available to us. It would be great if we could see opportunities, adversities, and ourselves more clearly. Unfortunately many mirrors available to us (advisors, loved ones, society, teachers, etcetera) cannot or will not provide an undistorted well-lit perspective. Most people offering to be our mirrors are biased or clouded or reflect a distorted perspective even when they don't mean to do so.

**Art and music are powerful. They trigger epiphanies.
They bridge chasms between people and ideas.
They shift attitudes and stir souls to action.**

Fool's Gold

The shiny new thing often turns out to be made of "fool's gold" and it can distract us or take us down some dangerous path to our ruin. But sometimes there really is a shiny new thing that is solid 24k gold. Wouldn't it be great if we all could get a fiduciary level due diligence report before we take the risk of letting go of what we have? That would be an incredible advantage to understanding and minimizing risk before we let go and reach for that golden opportunity.

How Many Eggs?

My youngest son Jake and I were discussing "The Dilemma" when he was about twelve years old. Even at that young age Jake could understand many of the points described in this chapter. It came as no surprise to me that Jake had sufficient wisdom to suggest the following courses of action:

1. Reorganize the existing eggs so the most important or valuable ones were kept and only the less valuable ones would crash to the ground when letting go and reaching up.

2. Grab the goose rather than the golden egg hoping that she would reliably produce many more golden eggs.

3. Jake also suggested that the person in the picture could use a soccer technique to slide the golden egg off f his or her head and catch it with one foot. That way both the golden egg and the goose that laid it could be retained.

It didn't surprise me that a twelve-year-old could have so much clarity and recognize so many ways to derive valuable wisdom from this picture because twelve-year-old children tend to find letting go easier than many adults do. I encourage you to look at this picture often. You can share it with people and discuss it with them. Some of the most mind expanding and enlightening conversations I have experienced have evolved from that kind of beginning. Metaphorically speaking, the rest of this book is an undistorted well-lit mirror of sorts. If you are willing to see the world and condition you are in with greater accuracy, perspective, clarity, and sense of purpose, you will gain maximum value from this book. Your dilemmas will be more accurately perceived and that tends to make them easier to recognize as opportunities and to transcend adversities.

When you think about your role(s) as an individual professional or as a business in the lives of your customers, which of the following best describes you?

- One of the many ordinary eggs

- The golden egg

- The goose that produces golden eggs

Every second of our lives we can choose to play whichever role(s) we desire. We can grow ourselves out of the ordinary eggs category and elevate our importance, relevance, and impact with customers and strategic allies. How abundant and magnificent our future will be depends largely on that decision and how well we follow through with the execution of details.

Chapter Three

The Mythical Best Mousetrap

Ralph Waldo Emerson said, "Build a better mousetrap and the world will beat a path to your door."

The late great Mr. Emerson said that over a century ago. While I treasure Emerson as a very wise philosopher and terrific author, it is important to remember that he was not a successful businessperson. Unfortunately his statement was untrue then and it still is not true today. The uncomfortable truth is this; History has proven that even the best inventions, products, services, artists, singers, etc. need to be marketed in compelling ways if they are to dominate their niches. Commercial success today depends upon a combination of: *a)* How amazing your offering is; *b)* How unique and/or proprietary your offering is; *c)* Consumer accessibility; *d)* Affordability; *e)* Total customer experience during the shopping and buying phase; *f)* Support after point-of-sale; *g)* Scalability; *h)* Follow-through with next generation offerings, *i)* Viral ability (ability to be easily and widely spread by customers and pundits); and *j)* Customer perceptions and expectations.

Yes, market prominence and especially market leadership are this complicated. And complication is but one of the many perceived adversities that scares business leaders into playing small and accepting a market position that is average. Fear of and avoidance of complication that stops or limits others can be a competitive advantage for you if you choose to let it be so.

Many of the world's market leaders and most successful products, services, inventions, artists, singers, etc. are actually inferior in one or more relevant ways to direct competitors that are "better mousetraps" in some way. This is especially true when the owners of the "better mousetrap" fail to provide comparisons that balance emotional connection points with technical and tactical application points.

Most consumers today are too busy, undiscerning, untrained, or apathetic to create their own comparative analysis. They perform little, if any, real due diligence. Instead they follow the paths of comfort and least resistance, buying what is most emotionally comfortable and compelling at a given moment and easy for them to choose. Price rules the purchase decision for many people today, until there is a serious problem. They seem unaware of or unwilling to learn from history or those with more experience than themselves. So they must learn the differences between price vs. cost and value for themselves. Therefore, if you have an offering at the higher or highest end of the price range, it is up to you to differentiate it in ways that emotionally and intellectually transcend lower priced competitors. It is entirely up to you to provide price vs. cost and value comparisons, due diligence, risk vs. reward, quality of ownership experience, and return on investment analyses. It would be wise to deliver these details in ways that connect and resonate intellectually, emotionally, and perhaps even spiritually with your desired customers, clients, voters, or patients.

May I suggest the following as a recipe for success in the first half of the twenty-first century?

1. Have a transcendent mousetrap, i.e. product(s), offerings, services, etc. in at least three or four price segments that are transcendent, relevant and important.

Similar to how luxury automobile manufacturers, airlines, hotels, and cruise lines offer specific features and/or experiences at multiple price points.

2. Provide compelling messaging at each price point that balances emotional with intellectual comparisons and justifications. I call this "whole brain" messaging. Provide both brief as well as longer messages. Make it easy for people to buy quickly or to go as deep as is necessary for them to satisfy their curiosity and justify buying your offering. Give customers as much as they want and need to *Self-Discover* how your offering(s) transcend those of competitors.

3. Transcendence becomes commercially successful more easily and quickly when it is directly relevant in whole brain and/or "whole being" ways. Commercial success demands ongoing resonance and relevance if it is to be sustained long enough to optimize the equity value of your business.

4. Do not annoy your customers with inane policies, procedures and excuses for them. Insulting customer intelligence or forcing them into "programs" which are irrelevant to them or which have unnecessary costs is a rapid path to extinction.

In order to succeed right now, especially with higher priced offerings, you must demonstrate rather than merely claim that your offerings and customer experience transcend whatever the customer already has. This is about you proving, in whole being ways, that your offering is superior in relevant/resonant ways to what has been previously acquired from you or competitors and/or what can be acquired from competitors now or next. To achieve optimal commercial success, transcendence must be inextricably melded with relevance and resonance to the customer. Demonstration through a whole brain presentation is paramount, especially with higher priced and/or technically complicated offerings. It is critical that you present a truly compelling, intellectually and emotionally gratifying experience leading up to and throughout the entire customer experience. This includes after the point of sale.

The leaders of most markets are able to connect with customers/clients in one or more spiritual or metaphysical ways. Once you gain customers' trust and money, you need to prove to them that doing business with you is wise, effective and personally gratifying. Do this, be this and you will establish and sustain at least a prominent, if not the dominant, position in your market. Less than this will leave you in the position of being just another ordinary provider. Make no mistake about this; ordinary providers do not enjoy a significant degree of customer loyalty or large amounts of quality referrals. Ordinary providers do not have many discerning fans and they seldom, if ever, receive referrals that move them "up market." If you are not getting significant amounts of up market referrals, it is probably because your offerings are not special or compelling enough. In other words, it is an indicator that an offering is too ordinary to deserve "honorable mention" by customers/advocates who could otherwise give you referrals to ideal clients, patients, donors or customers.

Business conducted in this transcendent and relevant way can provide you with a massive increase in cash flow and the market leader position. That in turn translates into top of class equity value and *financial* proof that your life's work is indeed relevant and significant. If your life's work really is spiritually or metaphysically significant to others, they will acknowledge you in that way. Applying this recipe can lead you to prominence and it can provide you with true fulfillment in and from your work. This recipe is far better for people who strive for excellence than the typical "We do that too" business model used by the under-imaginative, the copycats and the pretenders self-determined to never even come close to being the market leader in their field. Some people are perfectly content with fifth through ninth place. They are where they are comfortable and that is fine for them. But I do not believe that is where you will find optimum financial rewards, personal happiness, significance or your best self.

Transcendent market leadership requires imagination, clarity of purpose, discipline and follow-through *constantly* focused on providing the customer with "Best in Class" offerings and a consistent elevated experience. Here is what you need immediately to transcend into and sustain market leadership:

- A transcendent offering segmented into at least three or four price points.

- Compelling attractive whole brain/whole being, multimedia messaging that wins the attention intellectually, logically, analytically, emotionally, and perhaps even spiritually of your most desirable audiences.

- A step-by-step process or system that converts curious people into paying customers in at least one price point. Think of it this way; Mom and Dad each buy an S class Mercedes. Then as graduation gifts, they buy each of their children a C or E class Mercedes.

- A client-centric customer experience that is so remarkable that your customers become your advocates and most effective salespeople. This is possible if you make it easy, natural, organic and fun for your customers to share the advantages and rewards of your offerings with their colleagues, friends and family.

I have broken this construct down into four very simplified main categories or market segments for you to consider as illustrated below:

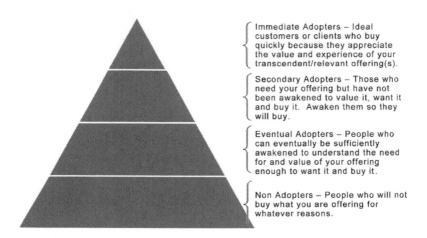

Immediate Adopters – Ideal customers or clients who buy quickly because they appreciate the value and experience of your transcendent/relevant offering(s).

Secondary Adopters – Those who need your offering but have not been awakened to value it, want it and buy it. Awaken them so they will buy.

Eventual Adopters – People who can eventually be sufficiently awakened to understand the need for and value of your offering enough to want it and buy it.

Non Adopters – People who will not buy what you are offering for whatever reasons.

One of the most important keys to success in this century is this:

You will convert more people into customers by making it easy for people to Self-Discover then Self-Select their own preferred ways into or out of your offering(s). Even if this means helping them get clear about how your offering does not suit them. The more people realize that your true goal is to help them make the best decision for them, the less "salesy" and self-promotional you will appear to be. When that happens, you will automatically be more attractive, even irresistible, to the ideal customers who are able to discern, appreciate, and pay for your premium transcendent relevant offerings. It is a paradox. The more people you help self-discover and self-select out, the more ideal customers you attract in and hold onto. You can attract more ideal clients who love and appreciate you and sing your praises. You can experience fewer complaints, returns, headaches, and avoidable stress because you will have far fewer unsuitable customers. This is part of the beauty of aligning yourself and your offerings with

Discerning people do not trust people simply based upon good intentions. Desired tangible results are essential in discerning markets.

what is relevant and resonant with your customers, clients, voters or patients. The best mousetraps today really do not have to trap anyone. The old sales schemes and closing techniques have long been antiquated in discerning markets.

As more consumers elevate into discerning customers, sales schemes, closing techniques, bait and switch tactics, etcetera, will statistically decrease in effectiveness. One way to easily transcend competitors who cling to those old modalities is for you to educate consumers so they become discerning enough to stop falling for those schemes. Elevating consumer awareness so they become wiser and make better informed choices is an excellent recipe for those with superior offerings and deliverables. Some business models, products and political constructs can only succeed in undiscerning markets. Rather than competing with such providers for those markets, you can choose to elevate the awareness and discernment of the people who typically fall for ineffective products, ideas and constructs. You can consistently provide free opportunities for less discerning people to choose to elevate their awareness and discernment. You can elevate people away from inferior constructs if you present your constructs in packages that matter to and resonate with those consumers.

Getting to the future ahead of your desired clientele by presenting them with transcendent, relevant, resonant offerings, which get them where they want to be next, is an excellent way to move yourself into market leadership. Go ahead and tickle the imaginations and desires of your most ideal customers. Give them irrefutable evidence of the better results your mind or imagination-stretching ideas, constructs, and business models produce. They will outgrow the offerings of your competitors.

Transcendence can be accomplished without attacking, defaming or being impolite towards competitors. Real results that are readily experienced are far more likely to go viral and remain viral than mere emotional rhetoric that inarguably keeps people in an undesirable status quo. Offer in every market you wish to lead a compelling and elevated view of customers'/clients' futures with you. This will automatically propel you ahead of competitors who do not know how to or care to create transcendent, relevant and resonant next generation offerings that produce the *tangible* result that is desired.

Chapter Four

The Tragic Better Mousetrap

As I prepared myself to write this book, I did in-depth research. I studied a variety of offerings that had become commercially successful and some that were underperforming or failing. That's right, it's possible to fail even when you have the best product or service. Businesses sometimes have the best offering, or the best mousetrap. But they don't always know how to position or sell their products in compelling, resonant ways that produce the visceral emotional reaction necessary to result in a purchase. Most people in this world are individually incapable of creating something transcendent and then driving it into optimum commercial or financial success. That fact is tragic enough, but even more tragic are the case studies wherein brilliant people have created transcendent offerings only to have them fail financially.

Enter Volkswagen's 2015 lineup of Golf automobiles. According to driving enthusiast magazines and newsletters, the entire Golf lineup for 2015 is transcendent. In each specific competitive segment, the Golf is measurably and subjectively above and beyond its direct competitors. I am fascinated at how mundane Golfs are visually while being so marvelous beneath that unexceptional looking skin. Sometimes this is true of people. The greatest athletes, lovers, leaders, and impactful authors can come in a package that hides the performance that lies beneath the wrapping.

In my quest to understand why Golf sales in America are so disappointing, I visited several Volkswagen dealerships and engaged salespeople and managers in discussions about Golf automobiles and the company in general. Not surprisingly, the "buyer experience" was well below what I have come to expect from Audi, Mercedes, BMW, Porsche, or Lexus. Not even one Volkswagen representative used language that would resonate with a driving enthusiast. Their presentations and responses to my questions were bland at best. Only one dealership had reprints of *Car and Driver* or *Motor Trend* articles that crowned the Golf as the award-winning car of the year and best in class. That kind of third party endorsement is much more credible and powerful than any brochure Volkswagen can create about its own products. As noted business development psychologist Dr. David Gruder says, "Kings and queens don't crown themselves. They are crowned by others." In this case the Golf has been crowned king by credible third party sources, but Volkswagen hasn't effectively honored, used, or capitalized on that coronation. Moreover the articles are beautiful, full-color pieces that would be inexpensive to reprint and make available to customers. Yet only one dealership had those reprints.

Apparently those responsible for placing the Golf with buyers lack the training or ability to appeal to driving enthusiasts in America. The most likely buyers of Golfs in America, especially GTI's, are driving enthusiasts, not ordinary drivers. Selling cars at the top of the price chart (where Volkswagen resides in their market segment) must involve presentations that are elegant and compelling. Not a single salesperson or manager used the word transcendent to describe their products even though they possess the transcendent product in each segment. How tragic is that? To have the transcendent product and not even use that word one time in a brochure or presentation proves that the salespeople and managers do not understand their products or who their ideal customers are. Salespeople are just about as competent and motivated as they are trained, coached, and mentored into being. Volkswagen would be wise to substantially upgrade the vocabulary and selling scripts used by their salespeople and managers.

I had so much fun test driving a GTI with the performance package that I *almost* bought one. The product is so good that I felt inclined to buy one even though I don't need another car. In spite of my enthusiasm, none of the salespeople were capable of inspiring a sale.

There are no tactical advantages to wrapping greatness or transcendence in an unexceptional package. Compared to Volkswagen, Mazda, Ford, and Hyundai are able to wrap their lesser mechanical products in better looking skin. Their products are visually more attractive, perform well enough for average buyers, cost less, and are perceived as being more reliable and less expensive to maintain. Being built in Mexico is a turn off for many buyers and until Volkswagen takes away the uncertainty of manufacturing quality and longevity, many Americans will prefer to buy products manufactured in

> Third party influence can be and often is essential for transcending the status quo or competition. Free third party influence is nice when it is given. You should have a plan in place that attracts third party influence for free. Don't rely solely on free third party influence, though. It is strategically wiser to also use a plan that connects your enterprise to high gravitas people that are paid by you to use their credibility on your behalf. Such people tend to have proven track records for deal making and the smartest of them are looking for ways to monetize their track records, connections, credibility, and influence. People like this can be priceless and they are nearly always essential for transcendence into market leadership. Once you learn how, it's not hard to find them and put win-win contracts into place.

America, Japan, or Korea. BMW, Mercedes, Audi, and Porsche all prove that Americans will buy products manufactured in Germany or their USA facilities. Volkswagen owns Audi and Porsche, how ironic is that?

Instead of a measly 36 month or 36,000 mile warranty, Volkswagen could provide a 60 month or 60,000 mile warranty. Or they could transcend Hyundai's 100,000 mile warranty. Volkswagen could also adopt a wiser, whole being approach to their business and marketing. Creating a soulful connection with driving enthusiasts will help customers become Volkswagen's best salespeople. Audi and Porsche have done so. Their customers have become advocates for those brands. Apple does so with its enterprise and its products. Volkswagen can too, and so can you with your products or services.

This is an excellent example of a company having the best mousetrap, but failing to transcend the competition because they don't know how to sell or capitalize on being transcendent. Volkswagen salespeople and managers are so attached to their banal, status quo way of thinking and talking that they don't frame their messages in ways that are congruent with the extraordinary products they provide. They fail on the frontlines, too by hiring average people to promote their exceptional products. Mundane people think mundane thoughts, use mundane vocabulary, live in mundane ways, and get mundane results. When they are given a transcendent product to sell, they can't sell it. They fail because they can't or won't think or behave transcendently.

Since people need to connect emotionally with a product to buy it, Volkswagen would transcend its competition by shaking off its use of average training programs, hiring average people, offering average warrantees, and using average vocabulary. They could do this by changing their messaging to communicate that car enthusiasts buy the Golf because ounce for ounce and dollar for dollar it is the best driving experience. They can prove this with the third party endorsements of the *Car and Driver* and *Motor Trend* articles. Most car buyers read *Consumer Reports* if they do any research at all. The last time I checked, *Consumer Reports* rated the Golf very highly. The additional use of third party enthusiast and "gearhead" publications would be new and compelling information for customers who don't normally read them. Helping customers view themselves as enthusiasts rather than as average drivers with mundane taste could elevate sense of self for those who can be taught to appreciate and value a superior driving experience. Like Audi and Porsche, Volkswagen could create a loyal following of people who crave more connection and resonance behind the steering wheel. Lifting people into higher consciousness and engagement is essential to market dominance.

Chapter Five

Defining Impact

Market dominance can be defined in multiple ways. Net profit, equity value, popularity (brand name recognition), repeat customers, market share and the volume or lack of unsolicited offers to buy your company, hire you, or elect you could all be considered. How much impact you or your company or brand are actually having in or on desired markets can also be measured in multiple ways. It might soothe your ego if I were to pander to you and tell you this:

> Measuring market dominance and impact is solely determined by how you choose to perceive it.

That statement is very comforting to a lot of people and it is popular advice offered by quite a few business consultants, advertising agencies, life coaches, authors, gurus, and mental health professionals. Such advice tends to relieve clients or patients and it keeps dollars flowing into advisors' pockets. But here is the simple unadulterated truth. That advice is unlikely to optimize the real tangible value of your enterprise or the optimum monetary value of your life's work. This book is intended for tough, mature, brave people who insist upon real, tangible optimal results. It's for people who have no time for or interest in pandering drivel that feels nice but separates them from excellence, prominence or market leadership.

In business, politics, entertainment, sports, and organized religion, impact and value of the enterprise are measured almost exclusively by some combination of numbers and dollars. Some small degree of consideration might be allowed for touchy-feely emotional perceptions such as customer loyalty, good will or beauty. But this is the bottom line:

It is critical that you fully understand, appreciate, accept, and take appropriate action on how market impact and equity value are measured in your desired field(s) of endeavor. If you make that your cornerstone and build your business upon it, you will be far more likely to optimize the income, market position, and equity value of your enterprise. Understand what discerning affluent buyers of businesses in your niche assign the most value to. Then build your business around that which they value the most, without sacrificing your sense of purpose and moral or spiritual values. Doing this empowers you to build a business that will magnetically attract the right investment capital, unsolicited buyers, strategic allies, and resources you need to optimize the value of your business and your personal net worth.

If you gain a trillion dollars in net worth but lose your soul along the journey, you will come to regret it. I have had a lot of meetings with very wealthy people that regret not being true to who they wanted to be at the core of their souls. Wealth without soulfulness, honor, respect, charity, and love will not make you happy and fulfilled. If you have the right mix of advisors around you, you can have great success, fame, and wealth and simultaneously experience whole being fulfillment, effective life balance, and far fewer regrets. You do not have to choose prosperity over spiritual well-being or integrity. You can choose to have all of the above.

Ten Goals to Transcendence

1 Nobody goes to jail. Our offerings are legal, client-centered, and highest integrity standard setters. We exceed fiduciary standards of due diligence.

2 Every contributor to our success receives a proportional win.

3 Our workplace has minimal drama. We are all courteous, kind, and professional and act like adults because we possess equanimity.

4 We honor our commitments. We do what we say we will do, when we say we will do it, and we achieve objectives within budget.

5 The world is bigger than our own budgets or checkbooks. Investment worthy/ready ideas can and will attract the capital and personnel necessary for success.

6 We attract rather than chase what we want by BEING what paying customers want and need someone to be. We are Blatantly Relevant, Resonant, Professional, Client-Centered, High Integrity conduits for our clients' happiness, success, and fulfillment. We are profoundly valuable to our clients.

7 Our client-centeredness is expressed by not wasting anyone's time or money. We are our clients' most trusted resource in our niche. Our way of being is imminently trustworthy and recommendable.

8 Our clients are our best advocates and emissaries. They refer us to their circles of influence because they are excited to have their friends, family, and colleagues enjoy the benefits of doing business with us. We do not ask for referrals.

9 Our businesses are a reflection of who and what we are. They are not who we are. We live balanced lives that keep us engaged with family and friends. We nourish ourselves intellectually, physically, emotionally, and spiritually to enhance well-being within ourselves and doing so sets a positive example for others to emulate.

10 Our businesses are assets that others will want to own. We are wise enough to sell our assets at fair prices and with reasonable terms so we can diversify and manage our wealth effectively. We always attract new and exciting ways to fulfill ourselves in business so letting go of a current business asset is not a negative. Letting go of a current business asset creates time and space for something even more rewarding next.

You can request a free, high-quality copy of our 10 Goals to Transcendence, suitable for framing from our website at www.TMLInstitute.com.

To be respected by discerning people as an authentic person you must live in alignment with who, what, and where you claim to be. You cannot "fake it until you make it."

In addition to professional or business impact, it is essential that you pay sufficient attention to and have respect for life balance. If you overly invest your time, talent, and resources on mastering the financial matrix of your business or professional pursuits and lose your morality, health, or loved ones, you will end up as just another rich, lonely, unhealthy, and out-of-balance person. Or worse, you will end up as another unfulfilled wealthy corpse in the cemetery. I implore you to establish a written plan for living a balanced and majestic life. Then be disciplined about truly living your life according to your plan. I know that people can be taught how to believe this is possible and then to use a plan to put that belief into effect. I have done so for myself and I have helped thousands of people do so in spite of the inevitable resistance encountered from within and from those around them.

Here is some irony for you — the most prominent regional and global businesses are usually owned by largely absent owners who delegate day-to-day management to executives that are willing to sacrifice personal quality of life and balance in pursuit of achieving personal financial gain and market dominance for their employers. Whether you are an owner, an executive, or employee, you do not need to be one of those self-sacrificing out-of-balance people. Be wiser and more self-disciplined about your quality of life. And here is the most unexpected aspect of this irony:

Absentee owner businesses are routinely far more valuable and desirable to investors and especially to buyers because this assures them that your business's continued success is no longer dependent on your day-to-day involvement. In effect, smart business people and investors are unwilling to buy "your job." They want to own the revenue and impact of your business and grow them bigger than you had been able or willing to do.

Working yourself into an early grave or into a rich but unhealthy physical, emotional, or spiritual condition is unnecessary and probably absurd–especially when you accept the truth of this paradox. Your business will be more profitable and valuable as it becomes less dependent upon your active involvement. So please make sure this is a key part of your impact plan and measurement process.

Chapter Six

Similarity and Unhealthy Delusion are Key Inhibitors to Maximum Impact

Similarity

There are scores of people who believe that the fastest and easiest way into your inner circle, advisory team, or pocket is by telling you how unique and outstanding you and your offerings are. For the most part, pandering is often effective for them, but it is rarely if ever good for their clients and it is not effective for anyone dedicated to excellence and market leadership. Before we go any further with this, please carefully study these definitions:

Unique:

1. being the first of its kind or being the only one of its kind

2. being without a like or equal

Outstanding:

1. prominent; conspicuous; striking

2. marked by superiority or distinction; excellent; distinguished

Please, for the sake of your own edification and clarity, answer the following questions in the clearest most articulate way that you can:

In what ways are you unique as a professional?

_____

_____

_____

In what ways are your offerings unique?

_____

_____

_____

What are the three most outstanding characteristics you demonstrate as a professional?

_____

_____

_____

What are the three most outstanding characteristics you demonstrate as a person?

_____

_____

_____

What are the three most outstanding characteristics your enterprise demonstrates?

_____

_____

_____

What are the three most outstanding aspects of your business or your off rings?

_____

_____

_____

Unhealthy Delusion

Being honest with yourself is a critically important step towards achieving mastery as a professional and aligning your enterprise with the #1 position as market leader. If you and your offerings are not unique or exceptional, you will not achieve, nor will you be able to sustain, market leadership. Believing that you or your offerings are more unique than you or they actually are is an unhealthy form of delusion. Do not allow unhealthy delusion to separate you from market leadership. To achieve the goal of thought leadership or market leadership, that goal must be more important to you than warm fuzzy feelings and anyone's comfort or ego, including yours.

In this time and place you get to decide whether to live in a state of unhealthy delusion or to transcend it. Being delusional about who, what or where you or your offerings really are is a recipe for mediocrity at best and failure at worst. The good news is this:

Every single second that you are alive you get to decide what you believe and what, if anything, you will do about your beliefs. Every single second that you are alive the choice to act or not to act is up to you.

In order to achieve and sustain market leadership now, where you live today, you must out-innovate the thoughts and behaviors of every competitor in the space you wish to lead. Don't worry about the lofty dreamers who have creative genius but choose not to act on it. They are not competitors because their inaction self-eliminates them from consideration by consumers. It is up to you to transcend the imaginations and the consciousness of your clients, customers, patients, constituents, and strategic partners. You choose whether you will actually become and continue to be unique and amazing in ways that are relevant to your desired market. This is how to play big rather than small. This is where you get clear about acknowledging, accepting, declaring, and stepping into your greatness.

The more similar you seem, the less interesting and attractive you are. The more unhealthy delusion you hold, the fewer people you will resonate with and the less successful you will be. The more you believe and trust in "yes men" and panderers, the more you separate yourself from discerning people and the more you distance yourself from your own greatness, success, fulfillment and market leadership.

Later in this book, you will find some current examples of self-destructive business behaviors. Market prominence or leadership is not just about what must be done to arrive and stay there. There are also certain behaviors that you must not engage in if you are to become and remain a market leader. For now, I offer you this:

> Be clear about who, what, and where your clients need and want to be next, then move yourself and your messaging into alignment with that before anyone else arrives there. Get there first. Occupy the high ground. Be the standard setter. Exceed the current standards. Repeat this constantly and you will be who, what, and where your clients want and need someone to be consistently.

Chapter Seven

History of Transcendent Ideas

History is full of transcendent ideas that failed to catch on and it is full of ideas that became viral and then dominant for some period of time. Many if not most transcendent ideas are not well received by the people in control of a market or society, or by the masses because they are beyond the imaginations and comfort of most people. The people in control want to profit and retain power by and through the status quo or the manipulation of it. In many cases genius or brilliance can only be recognized and appreciated by those whose awareness exceeds that of the controllers and the masses. Some transcendent ideas can only be appreciated by those who are at least brilliant if not geniuses. This may have been first observed when a prehistoric being decided to hit something with a stick or a rock rather than her hand. Almost immediately that idea caught on with most, but not all, "people." Inevitably there were some who resisted the innovation in favor of the familiar albeit painful status quo. Eventually using "tools" went viral and "people" everywhere were using them to good effect. Even if most "people" were not actually any smarter, at least more of them were acting smarter.

Eventually, bronze tools surpassed simple sticks and rocks. Transcendent ideas about the natural world led people to explore and experiment with combinations of metals and heat to create tools made of iron and then steel. Merchants and metal workers trading in bronze either adapted to new technologies and materials or they went out of business. Scientists studied and experimented with gravity, electricity, and the development of mathematics to understand and predict the movement of the earth and heavenly bodies. Their discoveries were seldom well received. Sometimes the people who introduce transcendent ideas are threatened and intimidated into silence by lovers of the status quo. Defenders and lovers of the status quo or comfort are the most commonly encountered impediments to growth towards personal excellence and market dominance. People operating in an under-imaginative overly-safety concerned way seem to be personally incapable of transcendent thought, at least temporarily. And all too often, they seek to kill transcendent thought as quickly as possible.

As you express innovative ideas you are likely to experience resistance from status quo supporters. The saddest aspect of this is that many of the people dismissing or crushing your ideas are those close to you. Some of the people you love the most or that are very important to you now are likely to increase their attempts to throw up roadblocks to impede your rise to greatness. Parents, siblings, friends, colleagues, your boss, and even people who would gain a great deal if your idea led to success are likely to discourage you. Some will do so proactively and openly while others will resist passively and secretly. This happened to Elvis Presley when the girl he was in love with and her family discouraged him from pursuing his music. Elvis had to decide whether to follow the immediacy of his heart and preserve his relationship with his girlfriend or choose to follow his passion, fully develop his musical talents, and fulfill his destiny.

Surprisingly, sometimes people who are unhappy with the status quo will sabotage anyone or every idea or invention that threatens to antiquate the current condition. Even people who are absolutely miserable in the current condition will sometimes resist the most effective solutions when they are perceived as being too far beyond their own limited imagination or sense of hope, faith, intellectual, or physical capabilities. Be careful not to underestimate the tenacity of immature minds that completely believe in the comfortable and popular myths of manmade safety and certainty. People fully committed to those myths will fight against the changes they fear and they are very likely to attack the messenger or change ambassador.

Imagine backpacking on a cold rainy day in a remote area and stumbling upon a group of Neanderthals who are about to freeze to death for lack of fire. Wanting to help, you pull out some modern day tinder and a windproof, waterproof match and easily start a fire to save them. While some might be amazed in a positive, inquisitive and friendly way, others may be so overwhelmed by the *impossibility* of what just happened that they might decide to kill you and then burn you on the fire you "created" with "Dark magic."

Sometimes it is wisest to introduce transcendent ideas a bit at a time. Especially if you are unwilling to let go of some relationships that are important to you right now. Scaring status quo supporters too much or all at once could get you fired or even killed. It could cost you your marriage if you do not go about it carefully. Instead of overwhelming the under-imaginative or those with status quo minds, you can introduce innovative ideas "one-bite-at-a-time." Later we will explore how to use self-discovery to speed and ease acceptance and avoid getting your idea killed. This is just as true at huge organizations as it is at start-ups. It is also true in personal relationships such as friendships and marriages.

For the last three decades, my firm has enjoyed numerous Fortune 500 and middle market relationships. We also like to help smaller companies and their owners, especially through our internet-based training at our Transcendent Market Leadership Institute (TMLInstitute.com). Regardless of the size of an enterprise, one thing is ever-present — some people will perceive even essential transcendent ideas as too scary. When this occurs, at least a few of those people will find one or multiple ways to fight you to maintain the status quo in which they feel safe and secure, even when they are not actually safe or secure.

Remember this; the status quo cannot and will not lead you to, nor will it sustain, relevant personal excellence or enterprise market dominance. Defense of the status quo inevitably separates you from market dominance. Or it will result in the loss of market dominance. The status quo is often the good that is the enemy of great. The status quo is the momentum that favors mediocrity and it seeks to prevent the next wave of ascendance and excellence from coming into being.

Status quo addicts and those who relish their positions within a family, company, industry, or government nearly always attack new ideas and their messengers, even when it is widely acknowledged that the status quo does not work well and is in decline. Those who are over-attached to the status quo will often say or do anything necessary to impede innovation if they can't kill it outright. Status quo devotees also tend to dismiss any good idea they cannot claim as their own. When it becomes evident that they do not have any exclusive innovative workable solutions, they will attack the messenger or those individuals offering the dynamic solution. The craftiest status quo supporters rarely engage in direct or outright attack. They often pretend to be supportive adopters of new wisdom. Instead of truly adopting the new vision or innovation, they tend to favor passive aggressive behavior. They prefer asking a never-ending stream of questions such as "What if this goes wrong?" or "What if this bad thing happens?"

They seem to have a lot of imagination when it comes to all that could go wrong. They tend to offer little imagination, ask few if any questions, or make any assumptions or predictions about what could go right. It may seem as if every element of optimism within them has been lost.

Phony adopters pretend to be in alignment with the new direction. They pretend they are doing their best to apply new skills, technologies, and customer dialogue while claiming "this new stuff oesn't work as well as the old stuff."

Those who are firmly stuck in the status quo tend to exploit every personal soft spot, fear or anxiety that you as a leader might have. They do so in order to prevent you from initiating any change that they perceive as a threat or discomfort for themselves. For example, they might say something such as,

Primary Personal Thought Leader

If you are to succeed in attracting and retaining discerning affluent customers, you must be their personal primary thought leader. If you also serve them in heroic ways, you will be their most appreciated and trusted resource. You will enjoy a rare level of well-earned loyalty. Whoever occupies the position of personal primary thought leader will be more blatantly dynamically relevant, resonant, and compelling than any competitors. This results in unmatched dynamic implementation, trust, and loyalty in both directions.

Dynamic implementation is essential for everyone's success. Clients must take appropriate action, on time and consistently. Every advisor, vendor, and role player must proactively, preemptively, and dynamically fulfill his or her responsibility. This two way street, between clients and professionals who serve them, produces consistent results well above and beyond what typical relationships are capable of producing. Transcendent proactive attention to details consistently acted upon are the foundation for massive success in this chaotic world.

"But wouldn't this hurt the children?" They might insist that you have not done enough surveys to determine if your customers would even like the new direction or offer regardless of how many surveys you have already completed. Or, if they consider you to be hesitant or fearful about investing cash, they will find ways to exploit your fear around and attachment to money. They will not use positive expressions about money such as, "Let's do an estimate for return on investment." Instead they might ask questions such as "How can you justify this enormous expense?" or "Can't we get this cheaper from someone else?" or they may just say, "I don't see how we can pay for this." One of my favorite common negative statements is, "Your father would roll over in his grave if he knew you were about to spend such an exorbitant amount of hard-earned money on something soooo risky!"

To be effective at rising above all competitors, you will have to either win over lovers of the status quo or purge them and replace them with people who love and are dedicated to the idea of ascending beyond existing circumstances, market realities, and competitors. A new different direction often requires a change in personnel. Albert Einstein stated, "You cannot solve a problem with the same mind that created it." In other words, you are very unlikely to move beyond current circumstances, market position, or voter participation, etcetera by applying the same ideas or thinking that led you into the status quo. The people who produced the status quo are rarely if ever the people who can imagine and actively move a family, a political party, or a company above and beyond it.

Love, loyalty, and attachment to people or traditions that impede ascendance may be the most common killers of ascendance, innovative vision, leadership, and personal excellence. People who confuse love with protecting people from their fear of stepping beyond the status quo risk being the architects of their own failure. It is often hard to find the right balance of love and loyalty vs. effectiveness when we are strongly attached to people who really believe they have our best interests at heart. Even when they make it obvious that they are inhibiting growth; or worse, perpetuating a path towards irrelevance or failure. That is precisely the kind of choice faced and decided upon by Elvis Presley. Don't be surprised when you are presented with such choices. My life's experience has consistently proven that as we ascend above one set of circumstances and personal or business relationships, we are presented with new people and relationships that are aligned with and resonant with our new, elevated level of being.

Love and loyalty can be like angels that help propel us to greatness or they can be like demons that bind us to mediocrity, insignificance, and failure. An uncommon level of wisdom, discernment, and toughness is essential if we arc to become aligned with and arrive at our full potential. Sometimes we must choose between the love and support of certain people versus the vision, mission, and passion that burns within ourselves. Perhaps it is the phenomenon described in this chapter that has been separating most people from playing the bigger role that is available only to those audacious and tough enough to choose mission and purpose over comforting relationships with people who are not striving for excellence.

Chapter Eight

Your Experience with Transcendent Belief and Behavior

Everybody reading or listening to this has personally demonstrated some form(s) of transcendent thought and behavior. You worked your way into clarity about what you wanted, e.g. the ability to read, then you transcended every doubt, fear, and adversity that could have blocked or restrained you. When a human being makes the decision to rise beyond current circumstances, there is often an increased awareness of external adversities as well as internal limitations or blockages such as personal flaws, doubts, and inner anxiety. But you have already pushed past such things many times before. So you now get to choose to believe whether or not you can engage in transcendence again. If you believe you can ascend to a better higher place, you are more likely to get there than if you believe that you cannot get there.

Heroes and heroines feel fear and doubt. They are aware of at least some of the adversities confronting them. What makes people heroic is their level of willingness to overcome or transcend emotions, perceptions, and real adversities that ordinary people submit to. My friends who have conquered cancer or severe injuries have not only transcended those circumstances, they turned them into points of transformation. A transcendent perspective empowers heroic people to transform adversities, injuries, and illness into gifts. If you have ever succeeded in spite of adversity, doubt, fear and unfavorable or even very negative circumstances, you have personal experience being transcendent and heroic. In order to overcome fear you exercised whatever courage, willpower, tenacity, faith, and hope you could muster. Your gift from that adversity was increased courage, willpower, tenacity, faith, and hope. Exercising those characteristics or qualities grows them just as resistance training with weights strengthens and grows muscle fiber enabling us to lift heavier burdens tomorrow. Because you have already done so, you can apply what you learned from past successes and failures and begin your ascendance towards market leadership right now.

We live in a world where lots of people like to categorize and prioritize other people. Neuroscientists tend to agree that categorization is a natural human instinct. Physical appearance is a largely subjective topic with multiple categories ranging from exquisitely beautiful down to extremely undesirable or as my old friend Matt would say, "That person looks perfectly putrid." As you read this book you will be tempted to categorize people into one of two categories such as: a) Willing to transcend, or b) Committed to the status quo. Either this or that. Only two choices. That is the preference of most people and it very often leads them astray or limits their access to possibilities and solutions.

I urge you not to limit yourself or others in that way. Growing beyond the normal human desire to categorize others can quickly separate you from this simple fact:

> Every human being capable of cognitive thought
> has experienced transcendent thought and behavior
> many times before, and if they are sufficiently willing
> they can do so again.

If you want to speed and ease your ascendance into personal excellence, mastery, or market leadership, please be wise and invite others to support you and benefit along with you. It is unwise for you to "play God" by deciding who is and who is not able or willing to collaborate with you. I urge you to find helpful and inviting language, strategies, tactics and tools to help people recognize the benefit or perhaps the necessity of elevating above and beyond the status quo regardless of how comfortable it might be today. Help them grow into the understanding that the status quo is the momentum for mediocrity and the resistance against growth and greater abundance. The status quo may feel safe when in fact it is sometimes the riskiest place to be.

Years ago I noticed this phenomenon of "playing God" and how detrimental it is for everyone involved. People who decide to "play God" do so to their own detriment because they don't just exclude the people they omit from an opportunity. They also eliminate layers of people connected to those whom they omitted. Of course it stands to reason that excluding potential allies, messengers, or partners is self-limiting and limiting for others.

I found myself so frustrated by my realization of this shortsighted, limiting, arrogant and demeaning behavior that I did something about it. I wrote an article entitled "Playing God." I give it to everybody that I invite to play a higher and better game. The article is a non-threatening tool that has proven to expand awareness and guide people to be more inclusive and less exclusive. Since this book is my open invitation to every human being on the planet to think, believe and operate on a higher plane, the article "Playing God" is available for free at www.TMLInstitute.com.

Once you really understand this chapter and the article, you will see this "Playing God" game being played all around you by people who are either: 1) Knowingly engaged; 2) Unknowingly engaged; or 3) Disengaged. If I were to write a thesis on this subject, I might get too focused on the people who knowingly "play God" in order to limit, control or diminish the unknowingly engaged or the disengaged. I am not a fan of coercion or manipulation and encourage you to avoid any such techniques.

Instead, I encourage you to focus on your ascendance to greater effectiveness and alignment with being the leader in your market. The following exercise will help improve your clarity and discernment to the degree you allow it to.

Please list three examples of how your "Playing God" in business has affected you:

1 _____

2 _____

3 _____

Please describe three examples of how your "Playing God" has affected your personal relationships:

1 _____

2 _____

3 _____

Please list three examples of how someone else "Playing God" has limited your success professionally:

1 _____

2 _____

3 _____

Please list three examples of how someone else "Playing God" has limited you in your personal life:

1 _____

2 _____

3 _____

It will not serve your own or anyone else's highest purpose or effectiveness to feel victimized or diminished. Blaming yourself or others for past wrongs is not going to elevate you or anyone else. The exercise is intended to open and expand your awareness of how humans limit themselves and others by categorizing, judging and prioritizing people even though humans are so incredibly incapable of doing so in a fair and accurate way.

The remedy is simple from my perspective. So I created this incredibly brief Macro Strategic Plan® that we use to guide our business every day. It is just a snapshot, but it will provide you with some clarity of our sense of purpose. You can use the formula to increase your clarity, purpose and direction of your business if you so desire.

Business Macro Strategic Plan®

Vision: Everyone capable of cognitive reasoning and action is able to elevate and exercise their inherent ability to think and behave in new and expansive ways.

Mission: Respectfully and politely encourage and help everyone who wants better outcomes to elevate their awarenesses of transcendent ideas and opportunities. Help them take effective timely actions.

Goals: Constantly increase our own awareness and skills so we become more effective at elevating ourselves and others.

Strategies

a. Attract as many strategic allies as possible.

b. Empower allies with media they can distribute to elevate themselves and everyone around them into greater abundance and well-being.

c. Actively facilitate the education of all willing students at price points that range from zero dollars to multi-million dollar makeovers/transformations for businesses, individuals, political parties, charities, and religions.

Tactics

a. Internet training

b. Internet group mentoring

c. Personal face-to-face, side-by-side mentoring

d. Direct mail

e. PBS television presentations/transformational events

f. Radio interviews

g. Television appearances

Tools

a. Books

b. Articles

c. Blogs

d. Audio

e. Video

f. All new and relevant tools for distribution

People: Employees, allies, partners, and all people who are passionate about and sufficiently willing to elevate themselves and others through the highest integrity methods known to humanity. No coercion, manipulation, deceit or force.

You may feel inclined to create your own mini Macro Strategic Plan® rather than use ours. I encourage you to use the fullness of your unlimited imagination or connect with people that already possess the proven ability and willingness to help you imagine and manifest the next and best version of your life and business. Consider politely disengaging from anyone who wants to exclude or limit you by playing God with you or your enterprise. More insight on this is available at our Transcendent Market Leadership Institute at www.TMLInstitute.com

Chapter Nine

Interdependence is the Fastest Most Effective Path to Success

In business we rarely have to rely solely upon ourselves as individuals to conquer adversity or to rise beyond where we are at a given moment. Conquering negative circumstances or insufficient financial resources, certain necessary talents, skills and capabilities seems easier in business. Effective leaders are more likely to hire, rent, license, or buy what they lack than they are in their personal lives. As silly or unwise as that is, most people fail to apply sound business principles such as comprehensive strategic planning, delegation of roles, and resource and priority management in their personal lives. Far too often, even highly effective business people tend to leave their business and financial acumen at the office. They often fail to apply them to their own net worth and/or to their charitable endeavors. They fail to treat their net worth as though it is a business unto itself. They often treat the enterprise they work for with more respect than the net worth of their own personal enterprise.

Even those with the greatest imaginations and capacity for creation do better when their ways of being are interdependent. Think of the most prominent players in any market, field of endeavor or sport. Each prominent player must rely upon several above-ordinary people in order to achieve and sustain success. One of my clients used to be a high level executive at a little company called Intel. According to him, that company's massive growth and success was more about the quality and capacity of its people and less about its products, or mousetraps. In the field of high tech, it is unlikely that any product can sustain dominance or massive growth. Every product, no matter how innovative or superior, eventually, and usually very quickly, becomes obsolete. Even a successive stream of super products is not enough.

Intel applied the principle of interdependence to become massively successful and dominant in its niche. It obtained and retained the most excellent people the company could find. Intel was sometimes accused of trying to "steal" the best and brightest from competitors so the company could populate every department or division with the most brilliant, dedicated people obtainable. The charge was unfair and immature and Intel's leadership refused to settle for mediocre people or their mundane results regardless of what was said. Mundane people tend to consistently produce mediocre results and seem quite comfortable aiming for and being ordinary. In fact, many mundane people tenaciously defend the mediocrity in which they live. Lots of people aim for a normal, ordinary job or life. So they usually end up awash in a sea of mediocrity and so-called normalcy. If that is what one aims for, that is what one is most likely to hit.

Effective innovators are not always the best or most creative geniuses. Sometimes innovators are simply the best at finding and aggregating "next gen" ideas and the extremely talented and dedicated people essential for market leadership. Sometimes that is the best recipe. If you do not have everything you need right now to become and/or to sustain market leadership, get busy finding or attracting and acquiring it. Be the company or person with whom the best and brightest want to associate in order to have the most significant impact and to get wealthy. Imagine and figure out what awesome is in your niche and become that. Grow yourself, your offerings and your company into that by attracting, buying, aggregating, and hiring the people and resources necessary to be the most awesome player in your niche. Do not allow anything less than this to be your reality. And remember what I wrote in chapter four about upgrading your vocabulary so you don't make the same mistakes as Volkswagen. Transcendent products and services require unusual, resonant language and packaging if they, and you, are to succeed financially.

Back in the mid-1980s I developed a process which helps successful business people *Self-Discover* how and why they are failing to apply sound and directly relevant business acumen in their personal lives. The whole construct and each part of the process are transcendent. Not only because the idea and process are so unique, but also because it is wrapped in the greatest teacher of all time, self-discovery. Business leaders, founders, managers, etc. who complete the process find themselves in increased awareness and control of their own lives. They become more positively influential with loved ones and colleagues. They become more masterful of their personal impact and effectiveness with their personal talents and with their entire net worth. Getting clear and masterful

> Many professionals such as CPAs, MBAs, lawyers, actuaries, investment bankers, etcetera tend to become so fractionally-minded that they seem not to use the EQ and spiritual aspects of their talent. I know many such professionals who happen to lead spiritual, metaphysical, artistic, or poetic personal lives. But for many it seems as though those parts of themselves shut down whenever they are within a three-mile radius of their office. Those who learn how to transcend that phenomenon and actuate more of their brain and themselves whenever working with clients will enjoy more fulfillment, effectiveness, and competitive advantages.

with one's own passions, purposes and missions in life and how to judiciously apply one's wealth requires a great deal of uncommon thought and disciplined action. It requires letting go of relationships, assets, certain toys, and insignificant distractions which distance us from the more free, powerful, significant, abundant, and majestic lives that we could be living. This is possible once we learn how to think and behave in uncommon ways. To experience a significant and majestic life, we must be prepared to live an uncommon life. We must let go of that which is insignificant and that which separates us from living majestically.

Just as most business leaders and owners are disconnected from and living out of alignment with what is necessary to be the prominent player in their niche, most millionaires are not living the majestic lives that are available to them. This is because their current levels of awareness, habits, and behaviors makes such lives invisible to them right now. Elevated awareness leads to better clarity, which can lead to being more specific about what truly matters so we can pay attention to important details. Such awareness also clarifies what beliefs, habits, and behaviors we must let go of in order to experience more significant and majestic lives. This is what universally leads humans to more desirable results, but only if and when we move ourselves and our companies into alignment with what we want next. We get what we want next by aligning ourselves with or becoming attractive to what we want next. It's a simple formula when seen in writing, but human beings rarely apply it as it needs to be applied.

Every intellectually capable and attentive human being is experienced, at least to some degree, with transcendent, heroic thinking and behavior. Some people are more experienced and familiar with it than others. The good news is that each of us can hire, rent, license or even buy whatever thought leadership, intellectual properties, expertise, new products, new revenue channels, and capabilities we need to achieve market leadership. That is assuming, of course, we are not too frightened or too cheap to confidently lead ourselves, our businesses, our colleagues, and customers in that direction. On the surface, mediocrity can seem easier and cheaper than transcendent market leadership in the short term. Doing something yourself is so tempting because it seems to be faster, easier and less expensive than delegating and trusting it to others. Many fall into that trap and thus they separate themselves from significant or rapid growth and greatness. Interdependence is the path away from being mundane. Mediocrity is the most expensive market position or way of being available to humankind because it separates everyone involved from living at his or her best. Mediocrity is the enemy of the majestic.

The following exercise is intended to increase your awareness of the many topics that impact even moderately wealthy people in the United States. The wealthier you are and the higher you or your enterprise ascends in greatness, the more topics will apply to you. I wrote this next observation in my first book *The Wright Exit Strategy; Wealth — How to Create It, Keep It, and Use It* back in 1996 and it is just as true today so it bears repeating:

The curse of wealth is complication.

Please do yourself, your family and your enterprise a big favor by rating your awareness on each topic as honestly as you can. Do not allow yourself to believe that these topics are random and need to be sorted into specific categories. I chose not to categorize them because there is extensive crossover in these topics. Please allow yourself to accept that these topics can be intermixed and integrated into different yet connected aspects of life, business, and finance because of life's complexity. Please complete this exercise no matter how few tens or even fives you write. The exercise can increase your awareness about how well you are being looked after by various people on your personal or your enterprise's payroll. Paying for A-level representation and being underserved is not a good recipe for success. If you need more copies of this exercise, you can download them from our website at www.TMLInstitute.com

Universal Rate Your Awareness & Experience
Please rate your knowledge of the following subject areas using the scale below.

0 = You have never heard of the subject.

1 = You have at least heard of the subject before.

2 = You have a vague understanding of the subject.

3 = You have been involved in some meaningful exploration of the subject.

4 = You could provide a reasonably accurate verbal or written summary of the subject.

5 = You could provide a very accurate verbal or written summary of the subject.

6 = You have firsthand personal and/or professional experience with the subject.

7 = You are considered by many of your peers to be the best local authority on the subject.

8 = You are highly compensated for your work in the area. Peers, friends and even competitors recognize you as being a national expert.

9 = You are highly compensated for your work in the area. Peers, friends and even competitors recognize you as being

a national expert, *and* not only do you have technical ability, but your total breadth of knowledge and creative ability empower you to apply your skills in a macro sense.

10 = You are considered to be an international authority and/or you are one of the top 2% of people in your field or niche.

11 = There are no elevens.

0-10

— Identifi ation and written articulation of your own life's purpose(s), mission(s), values and vision along with a description of your current condition, obstacles, restraining factors, and specific oals

— Macro Life Management™ Plan in writing

— Business and/or Career Macro Management, Entrance, Growth and Exit Strategies shared with and eff ctively supported by *all* relevant advisors

— Micro Life Management™

— Personal Relationship Management and Elevation Planning

— Assessment of 316, 321 and 338 Qualifi d Plan Fiduciaries

— Fulfilli g philanthropic desires through charitable planning

— Fiduciary level due diligence process for interviewing, verifying and selecting professional advisors, consultants, lawyers, accountants, and fiduc aries across *ALL* aspects of your business and fi ancial dealings

— Personal and/or Family *Macro Strategic Planning*®

— Goal identifi ation and problem recognition skills

— False or ineff ctive meme recognition and shifting skills

— Origins and impacts of manufactured consent strategies on your attitudes about business, profit , and self-responsibility

— Manufactured consent client strategies vs. informed consent client strategies

— Strategy and tactics diffe ences between tool-focused fi ancial services providers vs. fiduc ary-based fi ancial advice and services

— Psychologically savvy rapport-building and interviewing

— Assessing how teachable or paradigm-attached you are, your loved ones are, your advisors are, and your clients are (paradigm attachment disorder)

— Principles, strategies, and tactics for helping paradigm-attached people (including yourself) become more educated, open, wise, and eff ctive

— Strategies and tactics for helping yourself and others increase fi ancial acumen, fi ancial integrity, and fi ancial responsibility

— Wise wealth distribution to heirs; changing dysfunctional or overly simplistic perceptions, i.e. equal seems fair but is often unwise

— Legally sound stewardship principles for leaders, corporate offic s, business owners, fiduc aries, trustees, advisors, clients, and heirs

— Ethical principles for fi ancial fiduc aries

— Risks associated with adopting vs. avoiding adoption of fiduc ary standards of care and transparency

— Qualifi d Plans: DB, DC, Sep-IRA, 401k

— Special needs planning, trusts, transfers, distribution, and protective fiduc ary management for those who are physically, mentally or emotionally unable to protect and further their best interests

— Specific ad anced estate strategies that emphasize 'Living Benefit ' vs. 'Inheritance Benefit '

— Multi-generational planning; the creation and documentation of 100 Year, 200 Year, 500 Year and 1,000 Year plans

— Formation and administration of Asset Protection Trusts and various offsho e strategies

— Business succession planning within family and outside of family

— 664 Exchanges

— Limitations, disadvantages, and advantages of Living Trusts

— Social Security rules, regulations, and procedures

— Medicare rules, regulations, and procedures

— Use of Tax-Exempt Trusts to sell highly appreciated assets without paying capital gains taxes

— Business *Macro Strategic Planning*®

— Rollover and reinvestment of qualifi d plan assets, federal and state regulations, limitations and details

— Roth IRAs

— Avoiding the tax on qualifi d retirement plan distributions (voluntary or mandatory)

— Irrevocable Life Insurance Trust design and funding

— Premium fi ancing pros and cons leveraging insurance premiums

— 1035 Exchanges

— Rule 144 stock transactions, regulations, restrictions, and details for distributions and diversifi ation to lower risk

— 1036 Exchanges

— ESOP fiduc ary requirements

— Private equity mergers and acquisitions

— ESOP merger and acquisition strategies and tactics

— Public equity mergers and acquisitions

— ESOP benefits and pitfalls for wners and employees

— Proposed or recent changes to tax rates, deductions or exclusions

— College funding: 529 plans, UGMAs and trusts

— Long term care insurance pros, cons, and funding options

— Generation Skipping Trust parameters and planning techniques

— Trustee competency, selection, and administration — private vs. institutional

— Alternatives to qualifi d retirement plans that contain far less "fiduc ary" risk for business owners and board of director members

— Limited Liability Companies (LLCs)

— Family Limited Partnerships (FLPs)

— Grantor Retained Income Trusts (GRITs)

— Grantor Retained Annuity Trusts (GRATs)

— Grantor Retained Unitrusts (GRUTs)

— Qualifi d Personal Residence Trusts (QPRTs)

— Self-Canceling Installment Notes (SCINs)

— Private Family Foundations, Supporting Foundations/Organizations

— Gifting & Freezing strategies

— Charitable Gift Funds and Community Foundation Partnerships

— Trustee, Custodial, and Administrative services, assessments, oversight, and risk mitigation

— Captive reinsurance companies and their funding, underwriting, and policies

— Self insurance pros and cons vs. acquiring commercially available insurance pros and cons

— Tax fili g, tax projections, and related accounting services

— Income, Capital Gains, and Estate and Gift Tax reduction and elimination tactics

— Reverse dollar cost averaging

— Risk reduction through diversifi ation

— Captive insurance companies and their funding, underwriting, and policies

— Financing arrangements for business and personal needs

— Real estate sales and exchanges (IRC Section 1031)

— Global vs. local or domestic investing, real estate, equities and debt instruments

— Currency arbitrage

— Growth investment selection and ongoing portfolio timing and management

— Advocacy of fiduc aries (proactive vs. reactive)

— Income investment selection and ongoing portfolio timing and management

— Portfolio construction with equities, fi ed income, and alternatives

— Alternative investments: metals, art, collectibles, hedge funds, options, real estate, etcetera

— Empowerment and mentoring principles, strategies and tactics for teachable people as well as those who are paradigm-attached and resistant to learning, growing and elevating

After becoming a continuing education instructor back in the 1980s for various professionals such as lawyers, CPAs, fiduciaries, RIAs, Certified Financial Planners, trustees and trust officers, CLUs, etcetera, I realized that most audiences need a tool to help them get clarity about how much expertise they possess and can prove. I have developed a variety of

> **"Alone we can do so little;
> together we can do so much.** —*Helen Keller*

---

these "Rate Your Awareness and Expertise" tools for various audiences over the past few decades. Some audience members love these exercises because they realize how it helps them become more clear about what they know and what they need to learn more about. These exercises can inform people about what is actually being documented, benchmarked, measured, and acted upon. They help us realize who really acts in our best interests vs. those who merely claim to help us achieve key goals. This exercise helps us understand the universe of possible tactics and tools that might benefit us. It informs us about what needs to be done within certain time horizons, budgets, etcetera. Some people, especially professional advisors, almost instantly become defensive when offered the exercise. Some feel confronted by it and deem it to be an uncalled for challenge of expertise or integrity.

Heaven help you if you have advisors operating at that level of consciousness. Some people are so insecure that they insist they have been threatened or offended even when no threat or offense exists. It is important to be leery of those who become defensive when encountering a self-assessment exercise. As an employer or as a client, are you not entitled to assess whether or not you are being effectively and properly served? The wisest and most mature people I know are not offended by assessments or evaluations. In fact, they welcome them because evaluations are an excellent means for proving value, precision, and exceptional performance without looking or sounding self-serving.

Many years ago when the exercise had far fewer topics, I forced myself to be at least a level 8 on every topic. I was concurrently doing several other things: providing Macro Strategic Planning® and facilitation to extremely complex discerning clients, striving to be an excellent husband and father, and functioning as a champion volleyball player and coach. I soon realized that I was in an unsustainable position. As my holistic and micro awareness improved, the list of topics increased. Simultaneously, various tax court and legal decisions occurred making it impossible for any human being to rate level 8 on every topic and sustain that level.

My best logical choice was to let go of the idea that I needed to become and remain a level 8, 9, or 10 on everything. I embraced the principles that had helped me win championships as a basketball player, volleyball player, and football player. It was obvious that I needed to apply a team approach. To excel, I had to take less personal responsibility and trust more people to do what they were already great at doing. Shifting out of the wonderfully appealing, ego boosting view that I was incredibly knowledgeable and experienced at everything that mattered and into an interdependent way of being was essential not only to my own success, but also for my clients' effectiveness and success. It was essential for my own well-being and the best interests of my wife and children. Everyone involved was better served by my awareness and decision to become more interdependent.

Anyone who actually believes they can become or remain the market leader without the brilliance and support of many other people is in for an awakening. How painful that awakening will be is dependent upon the intellectual density and ego of the person about to suffer through the epiphany that awaits him or her. Interdependence is the only way to achieve and sustain market leadership in 2015 and into the future.

The exercise is intended to open people up to that reality. No harm, offense, or threat is intended. As you share this book or that exercise with others, people will reveal to you how ready and willing they are to align themselves and your enterprise with market leadership. Those who mistakenly believe that they can succeed alone are in for a painfully rude awakening... or two or three. Smart people will not want to participate in the expense, delays, or pain associated with the awakenings that await professionals who lack sufficient awareness and expertise. That is why discerning people choose well-seasoned professionals who already excel at playing well with others. That is what interdependence is about. True professionals possess the wisdom, team temperament, and expertise essential to the achievement of the desired result.

Chapter Ten

Relevant Case Studies

Market Leaders are always tasked with providing clearly demonstrated proof of their innovation, wisdom, and unique talents. Without sufficient proof they simply cannot claim their rightful positions as the market leaders in their fields. This is a challenge for exceptional professionals. B, and even C and D level players become good at mimicking what the A-level people say. They cannot consistently do what A-level players do, the way they do it, but they can appear to be and sound the same. B, C, and D level players will often even charge the same rates as A-level players, even though they rarely, if ever, produce A-level results.

Unfortunately most consumers do not have or use a due diligence process that ferrets out the pretenders and mediocre performers. So I invite you to adopt this simple truth:

> Transcendence must be easily and immediately provable and it must be relevant and resonant if it is to enjoy commercial success.

This irrefutable proof separates the extraordinary people and organizations from the pack of wannabe competitors and makes it obvious and easy for serious people to choose them. As Michael Polin, a market leader discussed below, said, "When you work with magnificent people, you must raise your own game if you want to get maximum benefit from their advice, strategies, tactics, and connections."

A handful of abbreviated case study overviews follows. You can go much deeper by accessing links in the text below to find more detail about each person or by actually speaking with the exceptional people featured here. How much understanding or awakening you will get here is mostly up to you. This is self-discovery and self-selection made available to you about as fast and easy as is humanly possible today. Please allow yourself to have some fun here. There is a whole bold new world waiting for you on the other side of where you are beginning from right now.

Teach Me China —
Michael R. Polin, International Law Firm

I have been involved in several significant projects that included either a Chinese partner or China's government, but such engagement was not always easy to accomplish. Michael Polin, a highly competent, transcendent professional, has opened China's doors to many U.S. companies. He began helping conduct business in or with China and its citizens in the early 90s. Engaging with China requires extreme competence in many areas, including cultural, legal, moral, financial, sociological, and strategic. Michael is outstanding in each of those areas. But he did not always know how to prove it.

When Michael entered his international approach to business in the early 90s the world was a different place than it is today. Americans were leery of Chinese companies and their government. Michael quickly ascended to the position of an A player in his field, but had not yet developed the tools to demonstrate those skills. Shortly after I met Michael he formulated his program to show his provable, relevant, and resonant transcendence.

So Michael created a publishing and training company called Teach Me China, and a companion company called

Teach Me America, both of which were built upon his decades of legal and business acumen and experience in both countries. They attract ideal, A-level clients (American, European, Latin American, and Chinese) by proving his mastery of his subject matter. Michael owns numerous copyrights, service marks, and intellectual properties that demonstrate mastery of his profession. At this moment, he has no real competitors. Currently Michael is creating a new MBA and EMBA program at the request of China's most prestigious university, Beijing University. He has also been retained to develop similar programs for a group of transcendence-minded Brazilian business partners. Read more about how Michael transcends his competition by exploring his websites at www.polinlawfirm.com and www.teachmechina.com.

Michael coupled his creativity and experience with the ideas and formulas in this book to prove his mastery and make it available internationally. In so doing he has attained his rightful place as the market leader. He has invited me to serve as an adjunct faculty member in his MBA program at Beijing University teaching transcendent Business Acumen in English along with Chinese translation. Our e-courses are attracting many serious entrepreneurs, innovators, and professionals who are very serious about innovation and using it to achieve market prominence. Eventually these courses will be taught in a wide array of languages covering a variety of timely relevant topics.

Will Snyder of WTC Services LLC —
The Entrepreneurs Competitive Advantage

Unlike the owners of most small technology firms, Will Snyder had grandiose dreams of massive success. He had a big dilemma, though. His competitors can and do offer the same hardware solutions, and some can compete with his custom software creation. Their market has little separation on pricing. Even though Will's competition cannot pinpoint his unique advantages the good news for Will is also the bad news for them. Will is a DNA soulful entrepreneur and he knows how to use it to his clients' advantages. Being an entrepreneur allows him to think in transcendent ways that only very discerning and success-minded entrepreneurs share.

Will's uncommon ability to help elevate clients' businesses allows him to mastermind longer-term, holistic solutions to support his clients as they grow into what they want to be next. Being a market leader requires constant innovation in the technology aspect of one's business. Leaders do not have to personally pay attention to the micro details, but *someone* on their executive team must. Will sees technology solutions the way his entrepreneurial clients see them and helps connect the dots that are relevant to their transcendence. Timely relevant wisdom is always valuable to discerning people striving to play big and get real results. Such wisdom transcends equipment or software. This is something few technology people can do, so they cannot match Will's value propositions, offers or deliverables. His ability to engage clients in tactful ways that highlight and prove his unique competitive advantages allow him to *attract* the A-level clients others must pursue. Read more about how Will rose above his competition with easily and immediately provable results, resonant messaging, and impactful activities at www.TMLInstitute.com.

Will already possessed all of his essential current entrepreneurial wisdom and skills before we met. A speech I gave resonated with him in part because Will was struggling to articulate his competitive advantages and he didn't know how to describe them to prove his value to clients. Our mentoring process drew his uniqueness to the surface so he could clarify it and articulate it in ways that truly connect with his ideal audience. Once that happened, Will began to realize success that had eluded him in the past.

Will started using the Law of Alignment to align his services with the greater wants and needs of entrepreneurs. Doing so automatically activated the Law of Attraction. These two laws work in harmony with one another and they do not work as well alone. Accepting this simple truth is far easier than living in it and most people will do neither. I began to search for universal truths such as these to transcend my abusive childhood situation. When I aligned myself with the beliefs, principles, and lifestyles of effective stewards and leaders, my life changed for the better. As I began to do that, I attracted more good role models and commenced my path to a more peaceful and happy way of living. When Will achieved clarity of purpose and learned how to articulate what he does that is special, he was able to: 1) Present how his firm is exceptional and rare in ways that are relevant to his clients; then 2) Use his strengths; and 3) Use the new more effective language we developed to resonate with desired clientele. That resonance has made Will's firm attractive to its most desirable clientele. Will's firm now attracts rather than pursues ideal clients. The formula we used with Will works for all who move themselves into clarity and sufficient alignment with what they want.

You can visit Will's website at www.WRSGlobal.com.

Proactive Business Growth and Exit Counsel — Scott Lochner

Scott Lochner demonstrates unusually high levels of business acumen related to optimizing the equity value of a business before and after putting it on the market. He's an excellent corporate lawyer specializing in mergers and acquisitions and the inventor of patented, real-world intellectual properties and technological solutions. He has successfully monetized them by licensing them to companies desiring significant and enduring competitive advantages. Scott is a rare hybrid of business and finance lawyer combined with intellectual property entrepreneur. He knows how business owners feel because he is a business owner. He knows how inventors feel because he is an inventor. Along with that, Scott is masterful as a lawyer helping clients in every aspect of business governance and finance.

I met Scott in 2007 and he immediately earned my respect by his demonstrated ingenuity and proactivity. He was obviously transcendent and relevant, but Scott had not discovered how to use resonant language to connect with enough A-level clients. By melding Scott's rare and considerable talents with better messaging, he consistently attracts clients that his so-called competitors must pursue.

Scott and I have collaborated on a variety of business growth, value optimization, and exit projects since that time. He knows how to manage the legalities of business finance, governance, mergers and acquisitions at a masterful level. He also operates at an extremely high level of integrity, saving clients a lot of money where most lawyers would seize the moment and gouge clients with excessive fees.

In fact I regularly use one of Scott's innovations: a Front Loaded Letter of Intent for business owners to give to potential buyers. The letter compounds the effectiveness of my Macro Strategic Planning® and Exit Strategy process. Scott's innovation applies to discerning business owners, leaders, venture capitalists, and investors as it produces a faster and easier path to finalizing a win-win deal and better results for everyone involved.

The relevant, timely, actionable, innovation needed to move a business into market dominance, or keep it there, does not usually come from CPAs, lawyers, or financial advisors. In a world where "Proactive Business Lawyer" is an oxymoron, Scott's intellectual properties and inventions prove his ability to think proactively and monetize innovation. Eventually every licensing opportunity, sale, merger, or acquisition comes down to negotiating ability, mindset, skills, and credibility. Scott's track record speaks for itself. Price and terms are both very important in mergers and acquisitions. The most experienced A-level professionals do not want their clients to be sued. What they get in regard to price or cash is nice, but what they actually get to keep and use without stress and hostility is crucial to their qualities of life. Peace of mind, well-being, and friendly relations are also important to the new owner(s), investors, and the employees. Scott's win-win approach maximizes results for his clients' while ensuring that all parties gain. Read more about how Scott applies his uniqueness to help his clients achieve uncommon results at www.TMLInstitute.com.

Gregg Haglund

Some creative professionals figure out how to run their own innovative businesses within a larger organization. Additionally, they must develop and serve their own clientele in order to fulfill and exceed revenue goals. Uncommon creativity is often called for to transcend the limitations set by organizations housing these "caged" entrepreneurs. Gregg Haglund was already transcendent when we met him, but he couldn't prove it in relevant resonant ways. Corporate policies that force limitations on thought leadership or individualism are usually set by organizations to reduce risk and protect themselves from negative press for the brand or legal liability. They use a one-size-fits-all compliance template for professionals to work within. That is precisely what stops a firm from becoming a market leader. Real thought leadership is essential for attracting rather than chasing discerning, affluent clients. People like Gregg with strong entrepreneurial spirits are tasked with finding ways to differentiate themselves from competitors while staying in compliance with a variety of corporate policy induced limitations.

Like many of my transcendent friends, Gregg started off as a client. His uniqueness resonated with me so powerfully that we began to work together to find ways for Gregg to rise beyond the limitations imposed by his organization's compliance template. Just as I had to find ways to develop my talents and movement towards transcendent being while living within the stifling constraints of my abusive stepfather's home, Gregg had to quietly develop tools that would prove his relevance and his uniqueness. It wasn't easy because it had to be accomplished in spite of the small thinkers within his firm's compliance department.

Together we found a way to walk the fine line of challenging the status quo while seemingly working within it. Since his model generates impressive revenue and attracts A-level clients, he is able to see and act beyond the mediocrity of peers and competitors. Gregg walks his own path within the confining walls of his firm. Gregg is leading an evolution with proven results. By being true to his own wisdom, honoring it, and making it accessible in a transferable form, he now attracts those mature-minded investors who somehow knew within themselves that there was a better approach. Mature-minded consumers/investors look for someone to be what they need. Gregg's article helps those clients find him and know that he provides what they want but haven't been getting. From here Gregg has only to decide how dominant he wants to be, determine the breadth of his reach, and what level of personal wealth he wants to attain. I am confident that he will continue to attract the right clients and allies.

Gregg distinguished himself from competitors by articulating his unusually logical and transparent investment model in an article. His keystone piece, *It Works Until It Doesn't*, has so much resonance among his current and prospective clients that Gregg, and his firm, are now enjoying significant financial results and elevated customer satisfaction directly attributable to it. He attained this result even though his perspective on investing contradicted his organization's archetype. Gregg's article continues to fuel his ascendance towards market leadership as a fiduciary level portfolio manager and advisor. Gregg applies his transcendent Way of being so effectively now that he is a target of acquisition for competitors that want to use transcendence as the means for moving into market dominance and staying there. As I wrote earlier, wise effective leaders know they can rent or buy their way into transcendence. Read more at www.TMLInstitute.com about how Gregg's transcendence into owning and using his wisdom and translating it into relevant, resonant materials attracted A-level clients to his practice.

It's important to get to your own clarity regarding how serious you are about achieving market prominence or dominance. Without clarity of purpose, human beings are quickly distracted by challenges or opportunities that move us away from our greatest goals and fullest potential.

All of the questions Gregg has faced apply to every business leader, entrepreneur, venture capitalist, investor, inventor, aggregator or creator striving for market leadership. How will you answer each of these questions for yourself?

How dominant do you want your business or yourself to be?

_____

_____

_____

Do you want to be dominant locally, regionally, nationally or globally?

_____

_____

_____

Will you allow your humility and or self-doubt to limit the scope and reach of your vision and goals?

_____

_____

_____

How much wealth is enough for you to feel sufficiently or completely financially successful and secure?

_____

_____

_____

How much wealth is enough for you to be financially independent enough to not need or want to work for more money and to live your ideal life and perfect calendar?

_____

_____

_____

If you are currently being restrained by narrow minded defenders of the status quo that inhibit you from becoming a thought leader or market leader, how much longer will you tolerate it?

_____

_____

_____

Is it conceivable that you might be able to live a more ideal life and perfect calendar right now if you thought about this transcendently? Circle one: YES   NO   PERHAPS

_____

_____

_____

Summary

Thinking transcendently is challenging. Each of the people featured in this book pushed themselves well beyond transcendent thought. They took relevant timely action and moved themselves into alignment with who, what, and where their desired clienteles want and need someone to be. Each of them faced choices and challenges or adversities featured within the pages of this book. Each of them conquered their natural desire for safety, certainty, and comfort. Each of them found and demonstrated sufficient courage, boldness, and tenacity. I encourage you to study them more closely at www.TMLInstitute.com. There you will find more details that can serve as a springboard towards your own growth beyond status quo and competitors. As you immerse yourself in the study of transcendent people of action, you will find it easier to elevate your own consciousness, relationships and outcomes. There are many helpful people waiting for you to find them so they can help you elevate into a bigger role or even into market leadership.

Chapter Eleven

Accessing Transcendent Ideas

Some people are born with unusually high levels of natural talent for playing musical instruments, athletics, drawing, mathematics, singing, cognitive linear thought, quantum physics, or empathy and compassionate service. Since my introduction to the Bell Curve decades ago, I have used it to help people visualize many ideas that can be difficult for portions of the population to grasp. Here is the Bell Curve in its universal form:

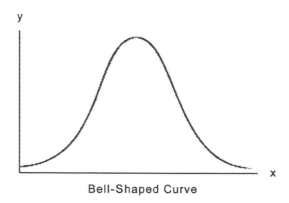

Bell-Shaped Curve

My brother-in-law Brent has Down Syndrome. He has an extra chromosome. When some people see him, they immediately think or even say out loud, "There is a retarded man." Because Brent looks rather distinctive, it is easy for people to treat him dismissively or even worse, some treat him with cruelty or indifference. Those of us familiar with people who have Down Syndrome tend to agree with the following statement:

> If you want to learn about forgiveness, gentleness, humility, compassion, and a loving attitude towards all living things, carefully observe the behavior of people with Down Syndrome.

Casual observers and those who choose to judge people based upon first glance or minimal interaction dismiss Brent and put him in the "retarded" category. They perceive only that which is superficial rather than who and what he really is. It is common and easy to categorize Brent as being on the undesirable side of the Bell Curve without looking deeper to find that Brent is a genius at the following:

- Humility
- Charity
- Compassion
- Loving others
- Sharing
- Kindness
- Intuition about when others need love or comforting
- Forgiveness
- Being at peace with life and everyone around him

So what follows is an unpopular, and some even say offensive, idea I began sharing with others back in the early 1980s. However unpopular, discomforting or offensive, it is a crucially important step we must take to understand transcendence to the point that we make it our way of BEING. Here it is in its most simple form:

> Every human being ranks on the undesirable side of the Bell Curve in certain categories. Every human being has genius within him or her that can be discovered and shared with the world to elevate, inspire or serve others. In crude language, every one of us is retarded in some ways while possessing genius in other ways.

I fully admit that I am significantly on the undesirable side of the Bell Curve when it comes to: 1) Technology; 2) Patience with inattentive, under skilled, or rude drivers; and 3) Diagnosing, fixing, or building anything mechanical. Because I believe that interdependence is the quickest and most reliable path towards effectiveness, I save myself and others a lot of anxiety by entrusting such things to people proven to be well above average in those areas. Whenever I desire a brilliant outcome, I go a big step further and I find masterful, genius-level people and entrust them with the outcome. I reward them financially and in non-financial ways that are directly relevant to them. I trust them with the micro details while measuring performance according to agreed upon benchmarks.

For all of his life, Brent will have Down Syndrome. Brent will not be a brilliant mathematician, piano player, singer or world class athlete. I will not become a gifted jet engine designer or software engineer. Both of us are fine just going through life focusing on our greatest talents and bringing to the world that which we have been gifted. We refuse to be limited by our so-called retardation or the superficial perspectives of the inattentive, shallow or casual observers who readily dismiss us as uninteresting, incapable or worthless. Brent and I are great buddies. We interdependently enrich each other's lives and the lives of those who are available to being lifted by our talents and gifts.

This chapter is intended to help you see beyond the limitations and superficial categories into which you or others have placed you. You can choose not to be defined or restricted by your lack of talent or skill in a specific essential area or your so-called limitations. You are free to define and elevate yourself through your personal talents or gifts. Everything you need to succeed is readily available either within yourself or interdependently through others who possess the gifts, talents, resources, strength, and experience essential to your success.

I invite you to find and honor that spark of exceptionalism that exists within you and give it breath. Doing so will empower you to play bigger. I invite you to transcend so called limitations whether they are tangible, circumstantial, mythical, real, comfortable or terrifying. I invite you to step into your greatness even though it will be uncomfortable for you and for some of those around you. I invite you to exercise, demonstrate and honor your gifts and exceptionalism so that others can be elevated by who you really are today and by who and what you are becoming next.

As soon as you begin living your life based upon your gifts and who you really are, it will be easier for you to recognize the gifts and genius within others. This will elevate you into greater curiosity that gives additional breadth and depth to your imagination. The more you apply your gifts, the stronger they and you become. Such growth is transformational. Living in such a state of imaginative and willing growth, you will begin to discover a whole host of people and resources with whom you can connect and excel. People who were invisible to you in your past level of consciousness suddenly become clearly visible and available to you. With each step

Transcendent ideas that can elevate you, prosper you, save you, and connect you to what is best for you, are always available to you.

---

you ascend, you become more attractive and you find more genius within yourself and others. As you progress within yourself, you will attract like-minded ascendant people to collaborate with or to teach you and mentor you. At this point in your development, your growth can become so consistent and rapid that results can be exponentially transformational. Sometimes you might even experience instantaneous results that you could not have imagined in your previous state of mind or way of being.

Accessing transcendent ideas is usually precisely proportionate to our personal degree of availability and openness to them. This is about our willingness being sufficient. Those who truly desire the abundant flow of relevant transcendent ideas will make themselves sufficiently willing and available. Then if you really want to grow, you must honor those ideas by applying them. Transcendent ideas that can elevate you, prosper you, save you, and connect you to what is best for you, are always available to you. However, it is very unlikely that you will find them within the status quo. The defenders of the status quo are likely to say or do whatever is necessary to keep you there because the status quo is where they are most comfortable. Some people are available and willing to be ascendant and transformed. Most folks are not interested in anything beyond the status quo and its relative comfort. Your big question is this: How available to transcendent ideas, behaviors, implementation, and the resulting rewards are you?

Connect with and honor your own spark of exceptionalism. Invite everyone you are connected with to join you. Doing so will open your eyes and ears, your mind and your heart to opportunities, connections, and resources that are currently invisible and out of reach for you. This will bring you access to transcendent ideas and people. You will become more interesting, compelling, resonant, and transcendent. You will become more attractive to success and successful people. You are invited to begin right now.

Chapter Twelve

Proximity to Genius and Transcendence

Proximity (nearness in place, time, order, occurrence, or relation) is a crucial aspect of human growth or decline. When we put ourselves in closer proximity to those who are already excellent or masterful, we make ourselves more available to be affected and impacted by them. This helps to grow us faster and bigger than we might otherwise be able to do on our own. One "throw away" or casual idea or observation by a genius or a master can be picked up by a student and used as a trampoline to reach heights previously unobtainable.

These days we have the internet and the cloud where we can gain access and perhaps some degree of proximity to more geniuses than what was possible when I was young. Throughout my adult life, I have continually searched for and found a volume of exceptional people who are already respected as being masterful in that which I want to learn or accomplish.

Using a martial arts analogy, when I was a white belt I quickly learned to follow the advice and example of the sensei (or master) rather than the free-flowing advice of well-intentioned beginners who were emboldened by their newly won yellow belts or purple belts. This decision saved me a lot of bumps and contusions. It endeared me to the sensei who took a strong personal interest in my development. He felt respected by me and he respected me more than those

> **❝I think for a lot of amateurs, their alignment is always out.** — *Karrie Webb*

students who seemed to flutter about taking instruction from Kung Fu movies, television programs, wanna bees, and gonna bees. My ascendance through the ranks (belts) was unusually rapid and I like to believe that I probably suffered less pain than I otherwise would have.

Today this world has more self-proclaimed experts than ever before. Amateurs, imposters, and downright frauds are prevalent on the internet and just about everywhere else. Nowadays it is possible to buy certain books and insert your own name as the author along with your picture and bio even though you did not actually write any portion of the book. In fact, you do not even have to possess any knowledge or relevant experience in the book's subject matter. Many so-called best-selling authors have bought and used internet courses which help authors achieve best seller status by merely selling a few hundred copies of their book between 2:00 a.m. and 10:00 a.m. on Wednesday in a book category where there is little competition or interest. Gaming the system is fine for the unscrupulous. Their victims are usually unaware that they are being or have been scammed until their money is long gone and their dreams or goals have suffered an avoidable delay. Self-proclaimed experts rarely guarantee meaningful and tangible results.

When I was a martial artist, nobody believed it was possible to progress from white belt to black belt by taking a one weekend intensive boot camp course. Today there are many such offerings available for just about any topic or field of endeavor. Simply stated, stay away from dabblers, wanna bees, pretenders, and imposters. Move yourself into relationships and alignment with well-proven masters who have the passion and the gifts essential to teaching. Not every masterful performer is a masterful teacher, but every pretender is a waste of your hope, faith, time, talent, and money.

Increasing your access to transcendent thinking and behavior is as simple as moving yourself into closer proximity (in person or virtually) and making yourself (intellectually, emotionally, physically, and perhaps even spiritually) sufficiently available to those who are already masterful at transcendent thinking and behavior. It is as simple as that, but of course it might be harder than you would like for it to be. If you come to the realization that you do not personally possess sufficient talent or skill sets to do this on your own, be okay with that. Immerse yourself in interdependence. Make yourself more available to the people and resources that are waiting for you to discover them. Seek and you shall find. When the student is sufficiently ready, the teacher that has been patiently waiting for him or her becomes as visible and as available as the student will allow.

A final bit of insight: When great opportunities, growth, and teachers appear, they usually will not show up as pretty, as easy to follow, or as comfortable as you would like them to be. Those that show up too conveniently all wrapped up in a pretty package at an incredibly attractive price, are nearly always an illusion, a distraction or a scam.

Like many critical aspects of transcendence, proximity can seem at least a bit contradictory and therefore confusing. As you shall see in the next chapter, proximity is also about aligning yourself and your business intentions with the kinds of clients and projects that bring you the most significance and joy. In business it is also important that you are rewarded financially in proportion to the value of the outcomes or experience you deliver to them. Sometimes to get to who, what, and where you want to be next, you can use proximity as a definitive strategy or perhaps as a tactical advantage.

Chapter Thirteen

Applying the Principle of Interdependence to Optimize the Value of Your Business

The most masterful prominent professionals in every field of endeavor have learned their craft by and through interaction with teachers, mentors, authors, and students. In addition, mastery is attained by actually performing well in a variety of circumstances. True masters can accomplish desired results consistently even when faced with expected and unexpected adversities. Mastery requires a willingness to think and act audaciously, independently, and interdependently. Achieving and sustaining excellence, mastery, prominence, or dominance is inextricably connected to our willingness to increase our knowledge and to act effectively as individuals and interdependently with other people. Even when some of the people involved are not ideally suited to the tasks that must be done. A person with the lone-wolf, overly self-reliant attitude, and good enough skills can become prominent on a small or local level. However, national or global market leadership in any business niche requires not only a strong, multiple-person infrastructure, but also an excellent external web of connections to highly effective people who are supportive of you, your cause, and offerings.

The vast majority of businesses today, even some very large and profitable enterprises, will die upon the death of their owners. Any business owner or leader wanting his or her business to escape such a fate must take preemptive, proactive steps to assure the viability and capacity for that business to endure for at least X years beyond the death of its founder or owner(s). It helps to have a plan to either sell your business when it reaches a value of X (your magic number,) or a 100-year or longer plan if you want to create a multi-generational empire. Here is a simple truth: All human beings including business owners, authors, leaders, inventors, and geniuses die. Businesses do not ever have to die. Death for human beings is inevitable; death for a business is usually optional.

In order to grow an investment-ready, merger-ready or purchase-ready business, owners or leaders must proactively develop that business with real-world longevity or sale/merger result in mind. Here is where this gets really clear. Investment, merger, or purchase readiness is completely provable through written, tangible measurements and documents. Businesses capable of enduring well beyond the lifetime of their founders or current leaders can also be proven based upon tangible, written, legal documentation, financial reports, and other mathematical measurements such as market share or position. Businesses either already are in an optimally investment-ready, transferrable, or enduring condition, or they are not. There is no hiding from this reality when presented with a negative crisis such as: A) a life threatening illness; B) a severe injury; C) the loss of mental capacity; D) the loss of passion to stay in the business; or E) the death of its founder/leader. Sometimes a positive crisis or opportunity such as an unsolicited offer to purchase that business at a reasonably attractive price and terms will appear. Of course the more prepared your business is, the more attractive to positive crises such as unsolicited offers from excellent buyers or strategic alliances it will be. Another typical positive crisis for businesses aligned with success is the attraction of very large business opportunities that demand growth of infrastructure. Both negative and positive crises stretch us beyond our comfort zones. Negative crises usually force us to respond. Positive crises usually give us the option to say yes or no to them. Sometimes what appears to be a negative crisis can be a positive opportunity in disguise. Many perceived negatives can be converted into positives when the right kind of imagination is applied or divine inspiration is interpreted and acted upon effectively.

Crisis offers owners or survivors the opportunity for sublime clarity. Generally speaking, you can wait for such crises to occur and be reactive, or you can be preemptive, proactive, and optimize your effectiveness early — as in right now. One choice puts you and the business in a very unfavorable state of being (reacting in negative crisis mode) while the other puts you in a favorable state of being where you are attracting what you want, influencing circumstances and people, and manifesting your vision of what is optimum for you. Yes, it is a choice all business owners and leaders are making every day, whether they realize it or not. Leaders who spend their days responding to brush fires are unavailable to the training, thinking, and focus essential to transcending the "brush fire" fighting circumstances they are immersed in. Most business leaders are lacking at least some of the essential training and mentoring necessary to see and act beyond the

I know about playing small because I once made the huge mistake of intentionally downsizing my expenditure of energy as a publicized thought leader. Others filled the vacuum created by my departure. Reclaiming my leadership position has proven harder than it was the first time around. I will not make such a choice again. I urge you to begin playing bigger immediately.

brush fire fighting aspect of their businesses. Most simply do not know what they do not know. That is why they are stuck where they are in an endless cycle of sameness, struggle, and separation from what is optimal for them.

Being, playing, or staying small is easy to do as an individual, as a company, or as a charity. Being masterful, prominent, or dominant on even a regional scale demands ongoing interdependent, proactive thought and action. In order to help people who want to proactively influence better circumstances and conditions for their enterprise, their family, or themselves, we have built a library of multimedia information and other transcendent resources created by proven, masterful people. This library empowers you to have greater access, proximity, and availability to A-level interdependence, transcendent ideas, and people to help you build the kind of enterprise, relationships, and life that you want. Visit our library at www.TMLInstitute.com.

Because of the demands on my time and energy, I cannot accept personal responsibility for teaching and mentoring everyone in every aspect of their lives and businesses. However one of my life's purposes is to help elevate you and as many willing students as possible beyond your current circumstances, incomplete knowledge, limiting beliefs, doubts, fears, and those people who want you to remain as you are and where you are now. I want to help you take relevant action and arrive at where you want to be next. Although it's a good place to start, even a library with thousands of articles, blogs, webinars, books, and courses will lack the human elements essential to your success. Proximity to masterful people dedicated to and invested in helping you overcome your obstacles and arrive where you want to be is essential for most people most of the time in most circumstances. And that takes us back to proximity and interdependence.

One of the ways I've returned to playing big is by using my

Plan your entrance, growth, and exit strategies at the same time whenever possible

interdependence to make my professional offerings more complete. To that end—or as I like to put it, helping you arrive at your best end in mind—I have formed a strategic alliance with two organizations that were built from the ground up. Let me tell you a bit about each of them. They can help speed and ease your success as a business leader.

Business Transition Academy

This organization was founded by Jane Johnson, CPA, CBEC, CM&AA, and Kathleen (Kathy) Richardson-Mauro, CFP, CBEC, CM&AA, precisely because they were personally acutely aware of the lack of unbiased training and advice available to help business owners and leaders optimize the value of their enterprises and gracefully navigate the complexities of cashing out or transferring their businesses to new owners, either insiders or outsiders, on their own terms and timelines.

Jane and Kathy have owned and exited multiple businesses in their careers. They found out through their own experiences just how much planning and preparation is needed in order to have a successful exit. Jane hired the wrong advisor to assist her in her first exit. That so called advisor was more concerned with his commission than helping her get the best price, terms, and conditions to suit her specific needs. As a former business intermediary, Kathy worked with over 150 business owners who wanted or needed to sell their businesses. Few of these owners had any idea how much their businesses were really worth and whether it would be enough, after taxes and fees, to fund their ideal lifestyles. Many others waited until some life event forced them to take action so their businesses had to sell for pennies on the dollar. This often happens to owners or their survivors when they have failed to proactively plan early and clearly enough. The sagest counsel I can give on this issue is this: Whenever possible plan your entrance, growth, and exit strategies at the same time. If you haven't already done this, you can begin now. Even if you have been running your business for many years, exploring your entrance, growth, and exit vision, mission, strategies, tactics, tools, and timing right now is beneficial. It exposes gaps or weakness and improves clarity, all of which are important to your success and happiness.

Jane and Kathy hold insightful, educational retreats for business owners who want to connect the universe of book smarts with real-world street smarts. Their specialized retreats and courses enable owners to get into close proximity with masterful professionals and other entrepreneurs and leaders with similar goals and timelines. Here is a partial list of what proactive thinking and acting owners can learn:

- How to clarify and create a meaningful life beyond the business;

- How much money they will need from their business transition to become financially independent;

- What their businesses are worth today and how to make them investment ready and transferrable;

- The pros and cons of both internal and external transition options and how they match up to owners' goals;

- How much owners are likely to receive from every possible transition option;

- How to develop a Business Ownership Transition Plan that includes a detailed roadmap and action plan to ensure success.

Owners who attend Jane and Kathy's retreats are choosing to be masterful and take control over their own destinies. They are choosing to achieve their own financial and non-financial goals. And they are choosing to prepare their businesses to carry on without them in order to preserve the mission, legacy, and careers of their dedicated management teams and employees.

I have agreed to make my books available as part of their curriculum and library. I have also committed to co-creating some webinars with them and to appearing live at certain retreats within the U.S.A. We are considering a more global approach for the Business Transition Academy via partners in other countries that want to offer business owners and leaders a truly unbiased source for education, mentoring and dynamic execution.

The Alliance of Merger and Acquisition Advisors

Mike Nall founded this resource in 1998. As a CPA Mike noticed that even some of the most prominent CPAs, lawyers, business consultants, advisors, and board of director members lacked sufficient awareness and skill sets related to business finance, mergers, acquisitions, licensing agreements, etcetera. Being an innovator, Mike saw the gap then built an organization and education curricula that bridges that gap by improving perspective and skill sets for professionals.

Becoming excellent at "herding cats" requires an unusual level of patience. Fortunately Mike Nall is an unusually compassionate, patient, and intelligent being. Managing the expectations and egos of ultra high achievers like some of those on his faculty and in his audiences or student body is not easy. Mike knows how to attract high achievers as faculty members and how to keep them engaged. This rare combination of personality traits and skill sets is essential to building and sustaining an A-level organization.

Mike and his faculty deliver extraordinary learning experiences online, at live symposiums, in classrooms at major universities, and even one-on-one with seriously dedicated students.

For many years Mike and I have collaborated and delivered speeches and webinars. In this next phase of our careers we trust the principle of interdependence more than ever. We are dedicated to attracting exceptional faculty and in-the-trenches experts who provide mastery of all the skill sets essential for optimum representation of business owners, leaders and boards of directors. Mike is one of the rare individuals who can understand and apply both the "hard" skills such as:

- Financial analytics;

- Deal making financial acumen;

- Deal negotiation;

- Corporate governance; and

- Change management.

And the "soft" skills such as:

- Emotional intelligence and connection to deal creation and completion;

- Spiritual awareness and connection to deal creation and completion;

- Multi-generational business succession considerations and planning; and

- Understanding the soulful attachment that many founders have with their businesses, employees, vendors, and customers to structure win-win transitions.

> "Trust is the glue of life. It's the most essential ingredient in effective communication. It's the foundational principle that holds all relationships. — *Stephen R. Covey*

In my ideal future, Mike and I along with Jane Johnson and Kathleen Richardson-Mauro are combining our thought leadership to elevate owners and leaders worldwide in every commercially viable language. In that state of existence, we cannot personally help as many people individually as we have in years past. However, technology expands our ability to attract owners, leaders, and advisors of every variety and connect them to higher more holistic ideas and solutions. In a way, technology allows us to be everywhere on earth, helping everyone who wants help to become more informed and discerning about their universe of choices *every* second of every day. By thinking and acting interdependently we help more people than we could as individuals. Our courses also attract advisors who are willing to step up their awareness and skill sets and be accountable for the advice their clients pay them for.

To live interdependently at one's highest level of effectiveness, one must have significant respect for time, talents, and resources. This applies to self and others. In every project our firm accepts, we are respectful of these issues with: 1) our clients and their visions and goals; 2) employees of transitioning companies; 3) professionals who are opting out; 4) professionals who are opting in and joining the project; 5) buyers/sellers/investors; 6) everyone's staffs; 7) strategic allies; 8) end users or customers of our clients; 9) vendors; and 10) the well-being and prosperity of our own personnel and business model. To make this as failsafe as possible, we decided decades ago that it is best to treat all of the above interdependent participants the same way we like to be treated. This is not always as easy as we would like for it to be. Some people do not operate at a high enough level of consciousness or self-respect and integrity even when it comes to their own vision/goals, time, talents, and resources. It stands to reason that people who do not sufficiently respect their own time, talents, and resources tend to be deficient at respecting that of others. All of us choose our own levels of respect for self and for others.

Being mindful and respectful with every human being, at the same levels as we like to be treated, enables projects to flow with greater ease. Wasting people's time, talents or resources is a fast track to failure. A-level professionals are not just active because they want to be profitable although that is a big factor. They also want to feel listened to, under-stood, and valued as human beings, not only as professionals. Masterful people demand proper financial compensation including cash and sometimes equity. They also like to be shown gratitude and appreciation in ways that are relevant to them beyond money.

I have had many business owners or top executives instruct me to renegotiate down a professional or vendor's fee without any respect to proportionality, value or balance. Make no mistake about this: A) some fees are non-negotiable; and B) fees that are negotiable should not be reduced to the point where any party ceases to be viewed and treated as an A-level client. The relatively small amount of money saved when disrespecting someone in that way very often results in a karma kick in the teeth somewhere down the road.

Some years ago I was matchmaking and mentoring two of my clients who thought that a strategic alliance between them could be quite beneficial. After a few successful telephone conferences, a meeting was arranged at the $100 million (EBITDA) client's office. Several top executives and two of the owners had divided up their day so my $20 million (EBITDA) client could tour the facility and become familiar with the business and its key people. This was a large undertaking and based upon time and resources, that day was worth over $200,000 in everyone's time and opportunity cost.

The morning of the meeting I was on my way to the airport to pick up the $20 million client when he called me and said, "Bruce, after finishing my pre-flight check and getting ready to fly my plane to the meeting, I noticed what a beautiful day it was turning out to be. So I have decided to put the meeting off and go fishing and waterskiing instead. Please make an excuse for me and tell them we'll reschedule for next month."

Demonstrating equanimity in that moment was a challenge for me. However, rather than feel angry and show that emotion, I chose to ask this client a series of questions with a patient and loving tone of voice. Within minutes we each understood a few things about each other. We both learned that the real reason he was not attending the meeting was that he was frightened and overwhelmed by the size and scope of the opportunity. He learned that I would not make up an excuse or lie to my other client. I canceled the meeting by declaring that the smaller client was not ready to have the meeting. The bigger client went on with its model moving closer to market leadership.

Even though the smaller client said he wanted to be a market leader nationally, when it came down to it he was not sufficiently committed to that goal. He was unwilling or unable to push beyond his self-doubt and fears long enough to show up for a two-hour exploratory meeting. The smaller client felt more comfortable being a small player in a niche that was more accepting of mediocrity. This is what suited his comfort level and it was the best fit for him at that point in his life and his way of being. Needless to say, no meeting was rescheduled as the maturity, perspectives, and goals of the players were misaligned.

I often hear people, especially motivational speakers, say, "Everybody wants to be successful." But the inconvenient or uncomfortable truth is this:

> Success demands of us uncommon levels of consistently demonstrated courage, toughness, and tenacity. Success demands of us an uncommon willingness to conquer adversities of all kinds. Success demands the letting go of attachments that would bind us to mediocrity and insignificance. Success is only available to those audacious beings that are sufficiently willing to transcend every doubt, fear, and comfort that would distract us from our purposes.

Earlier I used the word equanimity when I described how tempted I was to feel angry. We all feel emotions such as doubt, fear, anger, desire, expectation, etcetera, but I do not believe that we need to succumb to them. We do not have to sacrifice effectiveness with self or others just because some feeling shows up. Mature people, those who are truly dedicated to excellence and optimum outcomes, must immerse themselves in equanimity. Conquering our own and others' self-defeating emotions is essential to achieving and sustaining market leadership and it is critical to elevating personal effectiveness.

Being optimally effective at working interdependently with other A-level people requires uncommon levels of maturity, equanimity, and following through by doing what we say we will do. We must be respectful of everyone's time, talents, and resources. We must be on time, on point, and within budget. Doing so creates a fast track to enhancing credibility and optimum performance. It is essential for anyone, any team, or enterprise that wants to align with, achieve, and sustain market leadership.

Chapter Fourteen

Retreating Towards Success

By the early 1990s the consistent demand for my firm and I to provide corporate retreats, leadership symposiums, and author receptions became so great that we had to respond affirmatively or risk losing our prominence. As soon as a vacuum is recognized, someone will fill it, if it is commercially viable. Sooner or later, most opportunities are recognized and taken control of by someone. The point of wisdom is this:

> You get to choose whether or not you will be the one to seize and optimize the opportunities that you recognize.

We learned that tidbit of wisdom by intelligently observing how our most profitable clients dealt with recognizable voids. We also learned that at any given moment there is most assuredly someone planning and taking action to at least move up the prominence ladder, if not take over the most dominant position in every commercially viable market. To take this reality a step deeper into the metaphysical, every second of every day someone somewhere is imagining a transcendent offering and market condition that will antiquate almost every existing technology and expert or intermediary available right now. Someday a super computer the size of my little toenail will aggregate the sum total of business acumen, financial acumen, personal development, spiritual

> **"I find out what the world needs.**
> **Then I go ahead and try to invent it.** — *Thomas Edison*

enlightenment and universal wisdom available to human kind. That tiny computer will then dispense that accumulated wisdom to anyone willing to pay for it, anywhere in the world, every second of every day. That wisdom will be dispensed in the preferred learning media of each student or buyer in concise, easy-to-understand, and implementable sound bites and action steps. That will render people like me obsolete. Until then, I will do my best to help people elevate themselves, their businesses and their lives.

I do not know who it was that first formed the phrase "innovate or die." My guess is that it was uttered within a few hours, days or weeks following the creation of the word innovate. That simple statement effectively communicates this simple truth: Innovation, creation, change, and decay are the natural order of this universe. I truly believe that human innovation is inevitable; therefore, it is mandatory whether we want it or not. Naturally, innovatively-inclined people are not offended by such an idea or statement. However, even though I did not invent the construct or the phrase "Innovate or die," some immersed in or in love with the status quo have been angered when I've expressed it. I've even had a pencil, notepads, and a cassette recorder thrown at me.

One very prominent Silicon Valley law firm retained us to help its tax, trust, and estate planning division move closer to market leadership. Our firms shared a number of complex wealthy clients. The lawyers at this firm had worked closely with us and they knew that my firm Macro Strategic Design, Inc. ("MSDI") truly does not have any real competitors. Lots of imitators were attempting to mimic what we do and how we do it. However, because all of them choose to base their compensation on investment management fees, trustee fees, legal fees, accounting fees, or insurance commissions, discerning clients choose us rather than salespeople, imitators, or imposters. Once discerning people understand a firm's business model and compensation system, they quickly discover who is biased and who is not. Hidden agendas and revenue streams are revealed through sound due diligence of this nature. Our clients and other such discerning ones prefer that there be no hidden agendas and as little bias as possible. Hidden agendas, or even their very possibility, are unacceptable to discerning people wanting to optimize their results. Our imitators and imposters cannot seem to understand the importance of our absence of bias. That's because most humans see, hear, and understand that which they want to or choose to be aware of.

Since lawyers are bound by their code of ethics to understand, protect, and serve the best interests of their clients, their clients generally perceive them to be unbiased advisors. We Americans expect our lawyers to advise us to take action or not to act based upon their wise interpretation of protecting and furthering our best interests. This is how we want it to be. This is our expectation. In America and throughout most of the world, clients expect this not only from lawyers, but also from accountants, trustees and all who represent themselves to be fiduciaries.

Our retreats are multifaceted. They involve anywhere from three to five phases and we are meticulous in our discovery phase as well as in the other aspects of our process. Preparing our clients and ourselves for a one-day retreat requires that we interview department heads who will be attending or sending people to the retreat. Sometimes we interview every attendee in advance, then again later to follow-up and follow through. We conduct those interviews by telephone, in person or via Skype well in advance of the event. Following the preparation interviews, we prepare a jointly agreed upon agenda with clearly articulated priorities. Part of our role is to help the client recognize and include in the retreat agenda certain priorities that were invisible to them before we started. Sometimes the entire retreat is dedicated to one topic. Sometimes there are many topics. For that law firm, at that time, the main topic was this: Stop being treated like pharmacists.

As the retreat began, we had to help these lawyers recognize a variety of self-limiting constructs, memes and favorite talking points that would have kept them from gaining real clarity about their condition. People and companies, including law firms, charities, advisors, bureaucracies and politicians, often claim to have no idea how they ended up where they are, in an unwanted condition. But for us, it is usually easy to identify the language, business construct, and self-limiting memes and retrace the path they took that put them where they are right now.

In this case, 'Being treated like pharmacists" was demeaning to them personally and it was limiting their sense of significance and their income in lots of ways. They were stuck in a paradox. Their referral sources accounted for approximately 85% of their new business. Referrals streamed in effortlessly from life insurance advisors, CPAs, investment bankers, financial planners, trust officers, and a host of other professionals. These lawyers were viewed as exceptionally good tacticians and technicians. They were so excellent with technical details that they had transcended most competitors. They received many of their referrals from clients and professionals without asking for them. In fact, they had ascended to a level of prominence that was widely envied by competitors who were still stuck in the 'ask for referrals' level of awareness and behavior.

These lawyers all appreciated the consistent stream of referrals while resenting the limiting way in which they were being positioned by their referral sources. The following is how I recall part of our exchange:

I asked: What do your referral sources say when they introduce you?

The Managing Partner responded: They usually tell their clients that we are the premier estate planning lawyers in the Silicon Valley.

Me: But that is not the problem. What do they say or do that results in you being treated like a pharmacist?

Managing Partner: Nine times out of ten the referral sources create a financial or estate plan that they provide to their clients and to us. Then we are expected to write the documents and transfer assets as described in their financial or estate plan. It's like filling a prescription. They also quote a fee for our work. Thus they limit or eliminate our role in the discovery process. They eliminate us from the creative thought and planning aspect of the process. By limiting the scope of our work, they dismiss any wisdom we might be able to contribute and they diminish the value we could otherwise provide. Positioned as prescription fillers, we cannot use our talents, expertise, and wisdom in ways that benefit the clients.

Me: That bothers you because it limits you from doing the things that bring you fulfillment. That eliminates you from the creativity and wisdom aspects of the process. That delegates you to order filler and you hate that, don't you?

Managing Partner: Exactly! And we are tired of being disrespected and delegated down to order filler or pharmacist–especially when we disagree with the assessment or plan created by the referral source.

All of the lawyers interviewed during the discovery phase confirmed that this was the single most important thing we could accomplish during the day we were to hold the retreat.

Some clients are clear about who, what, and where they

want or need to be next. Some clients are in such a state of anxiety or pain that they really cannot achieve clarity about a positive future. For such clients, stopping the pain is the essential first step in clearing the mind, the heart and soul sufficiently to begin even imagining a brighter tomorrow. Just as a masterful surgeon works on the actual condition of the patient, elite golfers must play the ball from where it is located. In our business, our clients must always begin from where they are in that moment. So that is our starting point. We get "what is" rather than what is easiest or preferential for us. Such is the true nature of our universe. The following took place during the retreat which was phase two of the engagement.

Telling vs. Self-Discovery
Knowing how and why this law firm and so many others put themselves into such an undesirable condition offers me this choice:

1. I can tell them how they put themselves into this condition and exactly how to get themselves out of it and into where they want to be next; or

2. I can patiently and lovingly take them through a self-discovery process.

The more testosterone we exhibit, the more likely we are to choose option #1. This is what I call guy mode. It's when we choose what appears to be the fastest solution, even though in human relations fast is often not the most effective way to go. The problems with option #1 are:

a. People believe what they want to believe regardless of how ineffective or self-defeating their beliefs are.

b. Solutions provided by an outsider (in this case a person who is not a lawyer) can be easily dismissed with this idea and statement, "He doesn't know what he is talking about. He isn't one of us. He isn't a _____."

c. Ideas and solutions "not invented here" have little or no merit.

d. It's easy and popular to view the problem as external rather than internal. In other words, "Those dang referral sources are introducing me ineffectively. They are limiting my income and effectiveness."

Flat out telling a person that their problem is self-induced usually does not end well. Since we wanted this to end well for everyone involved, including their referral sources and clients, we took our students through the self-discovery process. They soon realized the following points had produced their undesirable reality:

e. They had neglected to teach their referral sources how to most effectively introduce them to qualified prospective clients.

f. They had yet to create a written tool I created called a Perfect Introduction that would make it easier for referral sources to know what to say and how to say it.

g. They had yet to show or prove how priceless they could be during the discovery process, the creative thinking process, and in providing holistic wisdom that was relevant, practical, and necessary for everyone involved.

h. When these eminently capable lawyers play the role described in (g), everyone's risk and liability can be reduced. Fewer mistakes are likely to be made and the probability for optimal results increases. But they had utterly failed to teach this to their referral sources. In fact, they could not even remember discussing it with any of their referral sources.

As we concluded this initial part of the self-discovery process our students were ready to grow themselves beyond their old ineffective practices with existing and potential referral sources. Next, they needed to self-discover how to:

i. Teach existing and potential referral sources how to most effectively introduce them to qualified prospective clients.

j. Create their written Perfect Introduction.

k. Effectively distribute that Perfect Introduction for maximum impact. In other words, how to distribute their Perfect Introduction so it magnetically attracted more referrals without asking for them.

l. Create at least 3–5 ways through which tactical mastery plus holistic wisdom could be demonstrated and proven to existing and potential clients and referral sources.

m. Create and distribute media to compellingly instruct referral sources about how including the lawyers in every phase of discovery and planning reduces risk and improves outcomes for everyone involved.

In this case, the why was simple to discover how to stop being treated like pharmacists and start being treated as sources of holistic, timeless, priceless, and relevant wisdom. One of the biggest challenges for many human beings who want to optimize impact with clients, colleagues, or family is frequently this:

Ascension, like success, is unlikely without sufficient clarity and wise, disciplined action applied long enough to have the desired effect.

Use patience and care to help clients self-discover their own best ideas, solutions, and practices or behaviors, rather than telling them what to think or do and how to do it.

To be effective with the statement above, we must put our egos aside. We must love our clients more than our own ego, comfort, and desire for speed, ease or profit. Those who possess and apply a fiduciary mindset and way of being will find this easier than those with a transactional or sales mentality and business model. Remember this idea: You get to choose your mindset, focus, and business model every single second that you are alive.

Phase three of this engagement involved follow-up interviews with each attendee to help them personalize and optimize their Perfect Introductions and develop timelines and accountability for following through with teaching their clients and referral sources how to introduce them more effectively. Like so many of our clients who fully invest themselves in this retreat process, these lawyers saw immediate and very substantial improvements in their sense of personal and professional significance and fulfillment. Several of them also doubled their income within the next several months. Becoming the author of the best life, business, or relationships that we dare to imagine requires us to look within ourselves. Clarity about what we do not want and what we do want is essential. It's important for human beings to at least consider the following construct.

The best version of you that you dare to imagine already exists inside of you. The best version of you is waiting for you to bring that part of you to the surface. As soon as you clarify who, what, and where you really want to be next, you will be able to articulate this into words. This will enable you to breathe life into the next and best version of yourself and your enterprise.

Sometimes a retreat, such as the one described here, is the most effective and rapid way to get clarity and develop an action plan that can be benchmarked. Some people progress faster when mentored individually. Ascension, like success, is unlikely without sufficient clarity and wise, disciplined action applied long enough to have the desired effect. Written action steps with benchmarks for time, income, profit, and market position articulated in writing enhance clarity and accountability. These things are essential for clarity about why we need to move in a better direction as well as when and how to get there. That kind of clarity is essential for real transformation. When this is all perceived to be self-discovered and self-determined rather than dictated by current leadership or an outsider, acceptance is far more likely. Ultimately, real success is self-determined. It cannot be dictated or mandated from ancestors, teachers, politicians, authors, or management. Success, like self-mastery, is what we imagine and define it to be. We either grow ourselves through clarity and actions that align us with success, or we do not. The choices that appear along the way are best resolved within our own minds, hearts, and spiritual perspectives. Because we decide our own choices, we self-determine our degree of alignment with what we want. This leads us to largely self-determined outcomes. These are essential points of understanding for anyone who wants to be a highly effective self leader and it is crucial for those wanting to masterfully lead a market dominant enterprise.

Retreats, especially those held off site where all of the participants are unplugged from the stress and hustle of the outside world, can be a necessary component of progression and elevation. This is an effective way to use outside, third party messengers to help you steward those around you to imagine and create their own way beyond the perceived comfort of the status quo. Combining self-discovery and third party messengers can be supremely important for your transcendence into market leadership.

Chapter Fifteen

Integrity Can Be a Transcendent Competitive Advantage

If you think you're leading at the level of your highest intentions, I urge you to think again. Few businesspeople have escaped being contaminated by the prevailing belief that being successful and profitable requires sacrificing — at least to some extent — personal integrity, spirituality, cherished relationships, ecological, or social responsibility.

Many of us are tired of politicians and doing business with businesses that have amoral or institutionally-centric attitudes. Employees are tired of working for executives and managers with such attitudes. Citizens are tired of government officials with such attitudes.

Hidden within this consumer-deep disenchantment lies a huge transcendent competitive advantage for leaders, owners, and executives with eyes to see and ears to hear. One that you can use to position yourself and your company as the integrity leader in your industry while also elevating your life, and the lives of those who work for you, to new levels of fulfillment and well-being.

Fortunate is a word that only begins to suggest how I feel about having Dr. David Gruder as a colleague and friend. In my opinion, David is the world's foremost assessor, trainer and mentor on the subject of integrity. Whether you use integrity as a personal differentiator or a business competitive advantage, David Gruder offers a variety of big picture (macro) solutions complete with detailed (micro) skills and procedures that help leaders, teams, and companies elevate into an extraordinary condition.

Being an extraordinarily competent professional or company without possessing and constantly demonstrating a high level of integrity has led to the downfall of a great many people who accomplished exceptional success. As immorality or amorality seem to increase, an integrity gap or vacuum has widened and deepened. People who have suffered at the hands of highly competent but dishonest self-serving professionals have begun searching for professionals and companies that provide high integrity plus extreme competency. The more discerning the consumer, the more value they place on integrity and morality. You can make this a transcendent competitive advantage. Low integrity professionals and politicians are constantly telling us how leadership and performance have little or nothing to do with personal integrity. The 2007 economic crash has proven yet again that professional competency absent integrity is disastrous for individuals, for businesses, and for societies.

Economic crash survivors and those still looking to pick up the pieces of their lives, finances, and business interests now value integrity more than they might have in the past. Smart high-integrity people the world over are searching for solutions and people that integrate relevant wisdom, competency, and high integrity. My firm collaborates with David Gruder to help those who see opportunity in bridging that gap, whether you are a consumer or a provider of services and products.

Together we have seen over and over again how individual lives, careers, brands, and businesses are improved and put on the fast track toward significance and success by elevating integrity. However, rarely is this type of improvement as comfortable or as easy as the other solutions that can be measured in financial or numerical terms. Integrity can often seem to be somewhat ethereal and it is a far more personal issue than many other things that can be measured simply with numbers. Because integrity is such a personal issue for so many people, it is very common for people to feel defensive about the topic. But openness and proactive engagement will move you forward where defensiveness will not.

This is precisely what sets David Gruder apart from other experts in the areas of ethics, integrity, and people smarts: he has translated culture creation from a vague concept that most leaders and businesses say they believe is important, into practical frameworks, skills, and procedures that make integrity and collaboration profitable.

A transcendent leader himself, he was the first recipient of a leadership award that was named in his honor in 2001. His subsequent six-award-winning road map for restoring integrity to all levels of society has been embraced across the political and religious spectrum, and with leaders in business, nonprofit, and political arenas. The range of categories in which his books have collectively won awards illustrates just how transcendent his work is: Conscious Business & Leadership, Social Change, Current Events in Politics & Society, Health & Wellness, Psychology, Mental Health, & Personal Development.

I'll reveal David Gruder's secret sauce shortly. But I first want to emphasize that while it is clear to me that integrity is a significant factor behind the numbers, I have repeatedly observed how uncomfortable it is for most people to willingly explore it deeply. Perhaps that's because, in the wrong hands, assessing a person's or a company's integrity quotient can sometimes be perceived as judgmental or confrontational. Let me be clear about this: those who want to succeed in the future, and then not lose the fruits of their labors, must be willing to perform due diligence on integrity as well as they would with numbers and business models.

As I said, most people with underdeveloped morality or people smarts become defensive at the mere suggestion that they or their company might benefit from an integrity assessment and skills or procedures upgrades. In contrast, people with very high moral standards are constantly self-assessing and they welcome credible third-party integrity assessment and training. They are not defensive about integrity no matter how uncomfortable the subject might be. They are proactive about integrity because they understand its immense market value. In fact, some are at last figuring out that being the integrity leader in their market is a powerful way to accelerate upwards toward overall market leadership.

During my career, I have seen companies increase their equity value by a full multiple or more simply by implementing integrity as a provable strategic and competitive advantage. I have even seen super high integrity companies completely overlook this as a strategy or competitive advantage when they and their advisors create advertising copy that describes their business and defines its value without featuring their integrity. Such companies miss an unparalleled opportunity to quickly realize an increase in their equity value by connecting integrity factors to financial performance data. Making those connections is rarely done by sellers, their advisors, consultants, accountants, or lawyers because it is outside the mainstream of consciousness. The professionals I endorse and prefer to collaborate with are familiar with my outside-the-status-quo views on the topic of integrity. Because of this, when the conditions are right , as when high integrity is already in place, we can figure out financial proof of how integrity makes our client's company more valuable, sometimes by a full multiple. Here is a simplified example to illustrate what I mean:

EBITDA	Standard Industry Multiple	Standard Valuation
10,000,000	X4	= 40,000,000
EBITDA	Integrity Multiple	
10,000,000	+1	+ 10,000,000
EBITDA	Integrity Enhanced Multiple	Integrity Enhanced Valuation
10,000,000	X5	= 50,000,000

Sometimes knowing what you have along with the wisdom, experience, and best choice of words or narrative to illustrate it, explain it, demonstrate it, and prove it in a clear compelling resonant way, is worth a lot of additional cash or earn outs in a liquidity event or exit plan. In the above illustration, the integrity quotient revealed itself to be worth an extra ten million dollars for the sellers.

My message here is that if you drive integrity to its fullest potential, it can become an essential strategic element of your competitive advantage that elevates you into your sector's market leader, whether as an individual, professional, politician, or business. Integrity can rapidly elevate your income, unsolicited referrals, loyalty, viral message distribution, and brand support. Improvement in any one or combination of these dimensions tends to elevate income as well as equity value. It also tends to reduce legal expenses, complaints, fines, and lawsuit judgments.

Even individuals and companies who already operate at exceptional levels of integrity can benefit from learning how

The vast majority of attempts to promote a company or person as being *high integrity* are ineffective. Too often the ad copy or bio uses language that fails to create a soulful or emotional connection. Directly claiming that you are high integrity usually puts people off and it can cause more distrust or skepticism than if you had not claimed to be *high integrity.*

to leverage integrity into a differentiating factor in establishing or retaining market leadership. High integrity business models and behavior also proactively avoid complaints and lawsuits. Reducing these risks and costly settlements can be an additional factor in helping sellers receive a higher multiple or more favorable terms in a liquidity event or exit plan.

My firm and David Gruder have a substantial track record for helping leaders, teams, and businesses with integrity in the ways described above. David Gruder's ability to elevate professionals and companies through high integrity practices that boost employee engagement and productivity as well as brand credibility is a real innovation in and of itself.

Business development legend Ken Blanchard wrote this in his kudos about Gruder's six-award-winning book on how to restore integrity to all sectors of society:

> "Leaders need an integrity check-up and Dr. David Gruder is just the man to do it. Too many well-meaning leaders haven't made the connection between their personal and relationship development and their effectiveness in the collective arena. Dr. Gruder's simple yet powerful integrity model provides a much-needed shot in the arm."

A number of other thought leaders have also grasped the value of integrity assessments, training, and mentoring. But we have gone further: We have made a mission of elevating David Gruder's breakthrough work to worldwide prominence. With that said, allow me to summarize the essence of his work, which combines a universal framework that integrates integrity and happiness, with key mindsets, skills, and procedures that make integrity profitable.

Gruder's study of sustainably happy people across cultures, religious orientation, and political affiliation revealed that they live their lives at the intersection of three core human drives that we are born with: 1) the drive to be who we truly are (Authenticity); 2) the drive to bond with others (Connection); and 3) the drive to influence the world around us (Impact).

His study of what creates sustainable integrity revealed that these exact three dimensions are responsible for sustainable happiness: Authenticity translates into self-integrity, Connection translates into relationship Integrity, and Impact translates into collective or societal integrity. Integrity isn't any one of these dimensions alone: it's all three in synergized integration and coordination. And the business applications of this are enormous.

Many find this illustration helpful for visualizing what this integrated approach looks like.

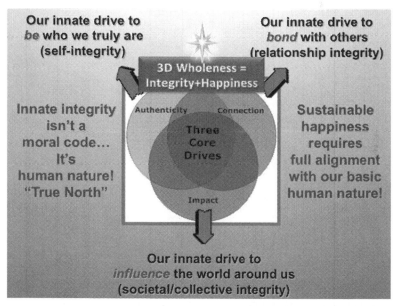

© 2010 Dr. David Gruder & Integrity Culture Systems | Reprinted by permission

What do the universal laws of 3D Integrity & Happiness have to do with achieving and sustaining Transcendent Market Leadership? In a word, everything. Consider this: According to Gallup's 142-country "State of the Global Workplace" study, only 13% of employees worldwide are sufficiently committed to their jobs to make positive contributions to their organizations. Even in the United States and Canada, which lead the world in job engagement, a whopping 72% are not engaged in their jobs. (http://www.gallup.com/poll/165269/worldwide-employees-engaged-work.aspx)

It doesn't take a rocket scientist to figure out the extent to which these levels of job disengagement damage productivity, profits, morale, loyalty, and quality of life. What seems like rocket science to the vast majority of business consultants and executive coaches, though, is translating integrity into learnable skills that build employee engagement, job satisfaction, and healthy corporate culture. Because Gruder's proprietary methods grow directly out of his framework for sustainable integrity and happiness, and because he is such an accomplished trainer and trusted advisor, the skills he provides are a vital key to Transcendent Market Leadership.

Gruder illuminates ways leaders and employees can express meaningful portions of their personal life missions by fulfilling their job's true value to the business, in service to the business's true value to its customers, specifically, and society in general. He combines the performance motivation this creates with the simplest possible blend of skills and procedures that maximize productivity, collaboration, and accountability.

Here is an overview diagram of how Gruder translates his framework for sustainable integrity and happiness into his secret sauce of practical skills and procedures that make integrity and collaboration profitable:

Integrated Keystone Mindset & Skills
That Make Integrity & Collaboration Profitable

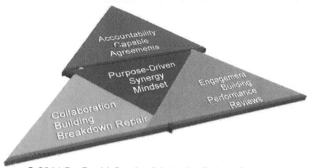

© 2014 Dr. David Gruder & Integrity Culture Systemize

I'm not going to describe here how David Gruder instills into businesses a purpose-driven synergy-centric culture mindset, or the training he provides in creating accountability-capable agreements, or turning implementation breakdowns into collaboration enhancement opportunities, or conducting mini and formal performance reviews in ways that maximize discretionary effort in the motivated (and help the unmotivated leave), or how to seamlessly interconnect these tactics to make the biggest difference with the least effort. Suffice to say, though, that few professionals, leaders, or businesses know how to do all of this in ways that actually maximize engagement and make integrity profitable. This is what makes Gruder's expertise so valuable.

As you may have guessed, my firm's transcendent contributions are in the nerdy practical, tactical details of systems and applications in boardrooms, valuation documentation, presentations, negotiations, and entrance, growth, and exit planning for owners, executives, and professionals. Dr. Gruder's transcendent capacity to help people professionally and personally elevate integrity behavior in profoundly practical ways is an ideal complement to my firm's strengths. His brilliance at helping businesses apply integrity as a means for increasing not only income, but also everyone's sense of significance, fulfillment, passion, and engagement... as leaders, managers, and employees at all levels in virtually any enterprise make his contributions indispensable.

David Gruder has graciously gifted his Integrity Audit assessment questionnaire to readers of this book. It will help you perform an initial self-assessment on where you and your business stand with integrity and collaboration as competitive advantages. You'll find it at www.TMLInstitute.com. You'll also find links at that destination to more information about Dr. Gruder's work, but I do want to mention a couple of his multiple websites here: www.DrGruder.com and www.HijackingOfHappiness.com.

Together, Dr. Gruder and I invite you to have fun with your Integrity Audit assessment. I also can't encourage you strongly enough to be proactive with integrity. Figure out how to make integrity an integral part of your personal and business success. Doing so will do more than just fill your pockets. It will fill your mind, heart, and soul with greater significance, fulfillment, and joy than you thought was possible throughout your enterprise and your personal and family life.

Chapter Sixteen

Identifying a Big Problem Can Create a Fortune for Those Who Dare to Solve It

In June of 2014 my wife and I were volunteers and chaperones who helped to oversee a re-enactment of an American pioneer handcart company. In total there were over one hundred and fifty people involved. We were responsible for accompanying ten teenage young men and women, every step of each day, striving for a glimpse of what pioneers experienced cross-ing the mountains before there were roads and civilization, as we know it today. Picture an oversized version of a rick-shaw-like cart made of wood, weighing about 500 pounds when loaded with camping gear, being pushed and pulled over challenging terrain at around 6,500 feet elevation in Central California's Sierra Madre mountain range. Trekking between five and seven miles each day was much harder than most of us presumed it would be. It was physically, mentally, and emotionally challenging for everyone.

When the experience became particularly strenuous, I reminded everyone that back in the 1800s, the pioneers did not have Gore-Tex raingear and many wore out their shoes or boots and did more than half of their 2,000-mile trek barefoot. Some were pregnant and many became so sick or injured that they died along the journey. We did not face hostile natives, bandits or deadly diseases. We did not hunt for food every day like the pioneers had to do in order to prevent starvation. We traveled several miles each day in good shoes with plenty of food and water. At best we hoped to gain a little insight into the adversities endured by pioneers and become more aware of how tough and tenacious the pioneers had to be in order to succeed in their quest. We all had to face and overcome our individual and collective human desires for ease and comfort if we were to rise above the challenges we encountered each day. That experience stretched us out of our comfort zones and connected us with levels of toughness and tenacity that many civilized people are not aware they possess.

Transcendence nearly always challenges our desires for ease, comfort, familiar faces, convenient circumstances, and the status quo. Such was the case when during the last rest stop on the final day I was presented with what has proven to be a huge opportunity to help millions of people first in America, then all over the world. As usual, that opportunity appeared wrapped up in a package that seemed inconvenient at best and like a lot of work at least a step or two outside of my immediate comfort zone. Since this opportunity involves multiple layers of complexity well beyond the daily awareness or attention of the masses it will positively impact, it is unlikely that personal fame will be a component of the reward. Many of the heroes and heroines involved in this grand adventure will most likely be unrecognized and perhaps even taken for granted. Some may be disliked or even disrespected in spite of their brave thoughts and actions. Very few of the heroes and heroines will receive much if anything in the way of additional financial reward. Sounds like fun. Please sign you up right away … right? However, this opportunity is special because it enables those who participate to elevate their awareness, discernment as buyers, and their effectiveness as leaders and stewards. It enables those who act upon this opportunity to prove they are willing to go that extra mile with due diligence and cognitive logical thinking to reduce

> *"To raise new questions, new possibilities, to regard old problems from a new angle, requires creative imagination and marks real advance in science.* —Albert Einstein*

risk, enhance safety, and protect millions of qualified retirement plan participants' hard-earned retirement wealth. This has a direct impact on every person involved with qualified retirement plans. Trillions of dollars are at stake.

There my wife and I sat on a rock at the final rest stop when one of the trek leaders (I'll call him "Dale") sat down next to us. As the small talk tapered off, Dale told me he was the committee chairperson for the qualified retirement plan for a municipal government and its many employees. He confided in us that, much like himself, there are tens of thousands of plan providers (i.e., business owners, executives, investment committee members, and others) aware enough of their predicament to feel overwhelmed by the weight of the liability of their fiduciary responsibilities. Dale went into detail about sleepless nights, then calling the hired experts seeking relief

People want to believe that all they have to do to avoid risk or to save themselves from disaster is to buy an insurance policy. That is wishful thinking at best and ineffective because insurance policies are not enough. Insurance policies will not protect you from government fines or disgorgements or lawsuit settlements that exceed the financial limits of the policy. Nevertheless, well-intentioned insurance salespeople unwittingly mislead clients on such issues because they tend to be under aware and undertrained. Match that with a wishful-thinking, delusional, under informed client and you have a disaster waiting to happen.

from that very real personal risk. You see, Dale and tens of thousands like him are not only underappreciated and under-compensated relative to the personal risk they have taken on, that risk or liability can extend well after they retire from their fiduciary role(s). This very real risk extends to every business owner and board of director member with every company that provides its employees with a pension or qualified retire-ment plan. The risk is largely underestimated and woefully misunderstood. Even by those who bear it. Those who do comprehend the risk are struggling to find financial safety and peace of mind.

Dale asked me: Imagine trying to do your best in an extremely complex area of business and financial acumen and then being sued for millions of dollars personally over things you did not realize you could have done (but did not do) by the very people you were doing your best to protect and serve. Imagine the fear of losing your personal net worth, especially after you are retired, and having to appear at legal hearings and depositions and reading negative stories about yourself in local or national papers. This would destroy just about anyone's peace of mind. Furthermore, if you lose that lawsuit, you could end up old and financially destitute even though you did not actually do anything harmful or wrong to anyone. The vast majority of people who agree to act as plan providers or committee members have too little or no under-standing of the risk they are personally agreeing to absorb. We are under-trained and ill equipped to take on such risk.

Dale went on to describe how none of the qualified plan experts seemed willing or able to do anything that would actually reduce risk for people such as him or the plan provid-ers. Instead of creating a risk reduction solution for their clients, most companies are choosing to take no responsi-bility or any actions to reduce that risk.

All my wife and I could think to do was tell him how sorry

Full disclosure is often a long distance from partial disclosure.

we were for his struggle. I went on to say something like, "I wish I could help, but I don't know how to help with that." Then it happened, Dale said something like this, "I heard that you are an expert on fiduciary issues." I responded, "Yes, but I have not focused on fiduciary matters related to qualified retirement plans." Dale suggested, in a good-hearted way, that perhaps it was time for me to learn more about this issue, the struggle, the anxiety, and find a solution. Dale was pleasant towards me and my wife and I wished I could help him. But clearly this was not my niche. I asked Dale how he had found out about my expertise on fiduciary matters and he told me, "When I came up here to scout the area I brought Joe with me. Joe told me his lawyers had hired you as an expert to help them prevail in a lawsuit against some financial advisors and so-called fiduciaries who had damaged Joe's family." I said, "I cannot discuss that case with you but those fiduciary issues are different than what you are dealing with." Dale's problem didn't seem like an opportunity for me. It looked and felt like a lot of work with little or no compensation for my focus, time, and energy.

A few weeks later I ran into Dale at a barbeque and we discussed his dilemma again. This time Dale said, "Bruce, somebody needs to solve this and you are the right person to do it."

People have been challenging me or inviting me to step up as a problem solver since I was a 10-year old elder brother parking my brothers before a TV so I could help my friend move. Arbitrating disputes on the playground expanded into me listening, understanding, and providing perspective to adults by the time I was about twelve years of age. That has evolved into finding creative solutions that solve complex problems or enable people to capitalize on opportunities. My companies and I have been doing this since the mid-1980s for business owners, executives, corporate leaders, multi-millionaires and companies with seriously complex challenges.

Sometimes my mind lets go of such invitations or challenges and then I go along my merry way working on whatever projects I have in front of me. For some reason I became interested this time, almost obsessed, with finding a risk reduction and quality-of-life improvement solution that could help millions of people. I was determined to find a tangible solution, not only for those in Dale's position, but also for the many millions of plan participants whose financial well-being is at risk. Dale's invitation had grown into something much larger than reducing liability or risk for plan providers, business owners, executives, and qualified plan committee members. The invitation seemed to come directly from the universe and it struck a spark within my soul. It had exponentially grown inside of me. I soon committed myself to either finding or creating a solution that provided significant wins for everyone involved. This would mean less risk because of better fiduciary performance, less anxiety, and enhanced well-being for all involved in qualified retirement plans.

If I could find or create a tangible solution, I could help millions of people increase their sense of financial security and peace of mind and improve their actual effectiveness. It could also be modified to apply to people in many countries that suffer because of risk and anxiety. The more I explored this matter, the more I realized that I was uniquely qualified to help anyone who lacks a fiduciary level due diligence process and the capability to tenaciously apply it. An honest-to-goodness fiduciary level due diligence process can truly reduce risk so everyone involved can enjoy greater administrative safety and real peace of mind.

One person's problem is often a
visionary leaders' opportunity.

Because I believe that invitations and awakenings such as this should be fully respected, I quickly implemented my long-standing fiduciary-level due diligence process to find a tangible solution. I figured that if I could find a solution that reduced risk by around 50%, I would have a positive impact on the lives of millions of people. That became my tangible goal: Reduce risk by 50%.

As I researched further, I uncovered this all-too-common problem amongst plan committee members who understand the risk for what it really is. A woman we will call Alice told me: Periodically my colleagues and I become so overwhelmed by the risk we endure and the anxiety we feel that we call for help. We ask the experts that the qualified plan is paying to help us remove or at least reduce that risk. We need a real solution. But what we receive is a conversation that feels a lot like some kind of child psychology sales script designed to comfort us even though absolutely nothing happens to reduce our personal liability risk or to improve safety for plan participants.

I knew that some companies involved with financial matters use partial disclosure of risk. This is commonly known as selective disclosure. Many financial salespeople and organizations systematically apply various forms of coercion and manipulation to win new clients and to keep existing clients loyal to them. Some companies hire psychologists to develop scripts for customer service representatives to keep clients on the books, paying fees as long as possible. I have found salespeople and their organizations to generally be unlikely sources for real fiduciary solutions. I have met some exceptional salespeople over the years who truly are knowledgeable about and dedicated to applying and living fiduciary standards. My intention is to attract such unusual people to join me in this mission to help those who are under-represented and suffering from risk that ought to be avoidable.

In my experience, most salespeople have only slightly more awareness about this fiduciary risk than their clients possess. They are taught and learn just enough knowledge to look and sound more knowledgeable than their customers and the general practitioner type lawyers and accountants who might review and otherwise reject the salesperson's propos-al(s). Most salespeople do not know how to think or act like fiduciaries and few enroll themselves in courses that would teach them how to think and act like fiduciaries. Almost none of them hold fiduciary credentials of any kind. Most sales organizations are doing too little or nothing to encourage or help their salespeople, consultants, or advisors to think and act like fiduciaries. I held enormous hope that I would find at least one existing fully operational client-centered and unbiased solution. If I could not find such a fully operational solution, I would either:

a. Aggregate some existing, partially suitable solutions or pieces into one holistic offering that would become the client-centered and unbiased tangible solution America and perhaps other countries need; or

b. Create my own unique fully operational solution.

What follows is the explanation of what I did, how I did it and why I did it the way I did it. Think of it as a type of univer-sal recipe that can be applied in any field of endeavor. This is important for you because it illustrates one possible path or recipe for you to follow as you bring to life a transcendent solution that benefits enough people to put many millions of dollars of cash flow into your pockets while increasing the market prominence and equity value of your firm. If you follow this recipe well, you can reposition your firm into being at least the thought leader because you will be helping solve some important problem relevant to your niche. One person's problem is often a visionary leaders' opportunity. This is especially true when there are millions of underserved and under protected people with trillions of dollars at risk.

Remember this: For thousands of years market leaders have known and taken advantage of this piece of insight on human nature. The most proven path to your own success lies in helping people get what they want and are willing to pay for. To get what you want, help others get what they want. In my story, people want less risk, improved effectiveness, greater financial security, and more peace of mind.

Chapter Seventeen

First Discover or Recognize the Opportunity, Then Initiate Dynamic Relevant Action

The blessing and curse of being recognized as a transcendent problem solver and opportunity optimizer is this; you are very likely to be in high demand. Lots of people will want to bounce ideas, opportunities, or problems off of you and most of them will want your solutions for free. You will soon discover, if you haven't already, that this universe is constantly presenting or exposing an infinite number of problems and opportunities. Since we mortals have limits to our lifespan, physical energy, emotional energy, talents, and perhaps even our intelligence, we must become discerning about whom we will work with or what we will work on.

My transcendent friends and I enjoy discussing the details of this combined blessing and curse and how to be discerning in the application of time, talents, energy, and resources. But this book is not about us, or the philosophy of such things. This book is about you becoming more capable at using and dynamically applying your imagination. Or if that is not working for you, this book will help you be more discerning when hiring appropriate people who have the imagination, audacity, and proven ability to help you and your business so that you can transcend all competitors. Some of the contents of chapters 16–18 could also inform you on what to do or how to do what is necessary to transcend the ill-at-ease mind regarding certain types of fiduciary risk that you probably did not know that you, your friends, or your clients are exposed to. So pay careful attention and use your imagination because regardless of what business you are in, the content of these chapters can be applied by you to elevate yourself into market leadership.

In business, recognizing an unmet or underserved need in a marketplace will not prosper you unless you, or someone who works with you, figures out exactly how to monetize tangible effective solutions or deliverables. In politics, it is quite different. History has proven that people with less than stellar intellect and morals can rise to power without a meaningful or positive track record for solving any problem or optimizing and monetizing opportunities. Politicians are rarely held accountable for their lack of effectiveness or their malfeasance in office. The economic crisis of 2007 proves this point. Business leaders and qualified retirement plan providers and management committee members are judged and often sued merely due to the appearance of underperformance.

Business people such as you and me are probably held to much higher standards of accountability for effectiveness in our job descriptions than most politicians or bureaucrats. Yet providers of qualified retirement plans and their plan committee members can even be sued for failing to do something that was unavailable to people at the time being considered by plaintiffs or government bureaucrats, who are looking rearward with brilliantly accurate hindsight. In our world, the most effective way to avoid being fired, sued, or prosecuted is to perform at a level that transcends the normal and customary standards of precedence or excellence in our field or niche. Rising above typical standards can go a long way towards discouraging lawsuits or getting lawsuits dismissed. At the very least, it can help you settle lawsuits faster and keep awards within the limits of liability insurance coverage.

Some Important Background

In the mid-1980s I was invited to serve as a due diligence committee member for a broker dealer investment firm. It proved to be a mind-expanding experience. That role empowered me to become aware of corruption, coercion, and manipulation that exceeded my wildest imagination. Within months my company was being pressured by investment packagers, insurance/annuity distributors, and even some of my own colleagues to remove me from that committee. My level of inquiry and follow through was more than some people could bear. Apparently viewing my role as an unbiased investigator seeking to protect our investor clients and my firm from under performance, unnecessarily high fees, flawed business models, and outright scams was too assertive and thorough for some people.

On the other hand, my fiduciary-type mindset and very detailed due diligence methods were noticed by honorable people who offered me the role of director of a Registered Investment Advisory (RIA) firm. At that time there were less than 200 RIA firms in the USA and by the time I was twenty-eight years old I had become a Managing Director of a very significant firm. Those two roles led me to comprehend fiduciary standards at very uncommon levels. Before I turned thirty, lawyers were seeking my advice on how to: A) successfully defend their clients in fiduciary lawsuits; and B) how to successfully prosecute companies and individuals in fiduciary matters. That background exposed me to a wide array of business models and practices as well as examples of coercion, malfeasance, manipulation, corruption, and negligence.

Within weeks of beginning this new endeavor referenced

in the last chapter, I found a nearly complete solution that already existed. The problem was that almost nobody knew about it because the companies that created the solution were not very good at explaining it. Their individual and collective messaging was ineffective because it was not sufficiently clear, blatantly relevant and resonant. Plus, they were very ineffective at sharing or distributing their message. This was, in part, because their message was very bland. Their messaging caused them to look and feel like everyone they were competing against. They had collaborated to create and deliver the best mousetrap, but their messaging and distribution were severely flawed. In effect, they were in a condition similar to Volkswagen as described in chapter four. Furthermore, a high level executive committee developed a compensation construct that was not as competitive as it should have been. Even the best mousetrap has to pay its inventors, distributors, salespeople, and service people fairly or it will not succeed.

It did not take me long to identify three immediate areas of typical, almost universal, administrative or fiduciary negligence and fiduciary breeches that nobody was addressing. Each area could be easily prosecuted in civil court. Furthermore, I believe negligence lawsuits on these subjects will nearly always be won by astute lawyers with expertise in fiduciary matters:

1. Failure to obtain a qualified retirement plan assessment from an unbiased non-conflicted provider of assessments paid for by the plan at a reasonable market rate. Most plan providers and committee members are negligent because they allowed the plan to pay a fee well below market rate to a company performing the assessment at a discount or at no charge. Many vendors will provide assessments at deep discounts or for free because they have something bigger and more profitable

to sell to the plan. Committee members who are duped into such an offering are in fact negligent in their fiduciary duty.

2. Failure to conduct a proper fiduciary administrative audit at non-discounted, market rate fees at least once every 36 months from an unbiased, non-conflicted CPA firm with demonstrable expertise in this subject matter. At best it is unwise to use a one-stop-shop accounting firm to handle your corporate affairs and to audit the qualified retirement plan. At worse it can be deemed to be negligent on the part of all those with related fiduciary responsibility. It is important for you to be familiar with arms-length regulations and best practices, then at least meet them or better yet exceed them.

3. Failure to conduct a regular (every 24-36 months) and thorough due diligence or selection process, often called a beauty contest, for all vendors associated with the plan. This would include Registered Investment Advisors (RIAs), 316/321/338 fiduciaries, CPAs, lawyers, investment managers, and consultants.

The government could also successfully prosecute these same points of common negligence on the part of plan providers. It became obvious to me that qualified retirement plan providers, committee members, and fiduciaries were not being sued nearly as often as they could be. If this discovery doesn't disturb your peace of mind, the impending surge of lawsuits certainly will. I had uncovered a whole new category for negligence lawsuits that plaintiffs, lawyers, and the government have yet to exploit. I expect that vacuum to be filled very soon by aggressively-minded bureaucrats and lawyers inside and outside of the government seeking to justify their existence, protect employees and plan participants, and to fill their pockets with fines, judgments, and disgorgements.

In January of 2015, I conducted a mastermind retreat with some significant long-term players in the qualified retirement plan business. When I explained my discovery of these currently unexploited gaps in the negligence lawsuits space, I estimated that 95% of all qualified retirement plans would lose such lawsuits. The unanimous consensus was: 1) my findings were correct; and 2) my estimate of companies that would lose was too low. The consensus was that nearly 100% of all existing qualified retirement plans, possibly including yours, would lose such a negligence lawsuit. Assessments, audits and beauty contests do not meet fiduciary standards unless they are conducted by unbiased, non-conflicted providers at fair market value. Assessments, audits, and beauty contests provided or conducted by undertrained, under-qualified or biased, conflicted parties do not meet fiduciary standards. It's that simple. In other words, a qualified retirement plan cannot select an investment manager just because her daughter and your daughter are classmates or teammates. Choosing a vendor based solely on size and reputation will not work. You must conduct a fair, unbiased, well-documented contest wherein all contestants are asked the same wise and effective questions. The answers to all of those questions should be recorded and transcribed and kept as records. These kinds of details really matter when audited or sued. Mastery of those details is the difference between success and failure. I also estimate that approximately 90% of those advising qualified retirement plans on asset management are too under-qualified to win a properly conducted, fiduciary-level due diligence selection process. I have been told that once again I am being too generous in that assessment.

Since this book is not about qualified retirement plan lawsuits related to negligence in administrative or fiduciary practices and behaviors, I will not fill these pages with the details. If you want to learn more about this and how to protect yourself, your company, and your clients, please visit www. MacroStrategicDesign.com and click on the "Stewardship" tab. The good news is this; once you learn about how and where you are exposed to this risk, you can begin to transcend that risk and overcome the enormous exposure that could ruin you financially. You can rise above old practices and deficient methods and greatly reduce your risk. Elevating your policies and behaviors above common standards is often an effective way to discourage lawsuits and mitigate risk. Being proactive and thorough with your due diligence will help you transcend the common coercion and manipulation techniques and earn your way into peace of mind. Well-earned peace of mind is far more effective for fiduciaries than blind faith in salespeople or their companies and platforms.

Here is a simple fact that I became aware of while in my twenties; the person or company who invents or sets a higher standard for customer care or the serving of underserved or unmet genuine client needs and wants has the natural and rightful claim on being the first or the best of kind. Sometimes those who set a higher standard might be held to an even higher standard than the one they themselves have set. Paradoxically, this can in some ways be the safest solution for those who want to reduce risk, increase safety, or improve performance. Raising the expectations of consumers can be like a double-edged sword because doing so:

a. Elevates you above competitors, which is a very desirable result;

b. Brings greater scrutiny to bear against those who set the new standard, which could lead to your downfall unless you perform a notch or two above the standard that you have shared with the public;

c. Invites far greater scrutiny on the myriad of competitors who are stuck in the status quo of the lower or common standard; and

d. When it comes to fiduciary or stewardship issues, those who can prove that they have taken every relevant and prudent precaution are less prone to lose lawsuits or to suffer fines and disgorgements inflicted by the government.

Exceeding the expectations of customers is far more likely when you initiate and provide mutually agreed upon written standards of performance for you and the client as well as written expectations of the customer. This is about you being proactive and seizing your own power to set the standards and therefore assume at least the thought leadership position in your market. Then, if you take relevant timely action and are tenacious enough and bold enough, you can rise into the market leadership position and an integrity leadership position in your industry.

For many decades, my firm Macro Strategic Design, Inc. ("MSDI") has used a best-of-kind fiduciary type due diligence process to locate and secure best-in-class professionals. MSDI rarely supports one-stop-shop" business models. We have found the vast majority of one-stop-shop models to be inherently biased even when intended not to be so. Discerning fiduciaries view those conflicts of interest to be too risky to accept. Instead we search the market for candidates rather than assuming all the best minds with the highest moral standards exist under one company name. Then we help our clients conduct a series of carefully crafted professional interviews. Although some refer to this as a beauty contest, it is really a Professional Capabilities and Dynamic Execution Assessment. We ask a series of questions that are welcomed and well responded to by true A-level professionals.

"I hire people brighter than me and then I get out of their way. —*Lee Iacocca*

These same questions are likely to be perceived as "attacks" and responded to defensively by candidates who are not fully ready to serve discerning clients or to deliver the highest standards of care and results. In common parlance, MSDI behaves as the tough interviewer so the client can have the more comfortable position of the nice interviewer. What matters to MSDI is the protection and furtherance of our client's vision, mission, purpose, and goals. How friendly or likable we may seem to the candidate is secondary to us and to our clients. We are always professional and polite, but someone must ask the tough questions and see through the mundane or even ridiculous answers that less than A-level professionals are prone to give. This is especially important when dealing with issues or projects where fiduciary standards must be met or exceeded. For the record, many of those mundane and ridiculous answers are common and often go unchallenged because most consumers lack essential fiduciary-level due diligence questioning capabilities. Simply stated, an over ly-simplistic due diligence process rarely if ever ferrets out unexceptional providers, pretenders, or scam artists who are inherently incapable of producing A-level results.

Our due diligence process and its questions are not feared by high integrity true A-level professionals. In fact, A-level professionals tend to enjoy being included in the fiduciary type of beauty contest we conduct because they realize that the majority of their so-called competitors will self-eliminate rather quickly when interviewed by us. Discerning people are not afraid of wise, provocative, and revealing questions. They welcome them. Such questions encourage growth, improvement, and ascension for them and their business process. Our

> **"Nothing can stop the man with the right mental attitude from achieving his goal; nothing on earth can help the man with the wrong mental attitude.** — *Thomas Jefferson*

process positively impacts both A-level professionals and our clients. Those who are eliminated during the process can choose to learn and grow from the experience by looking within themselves and demanding self-improvement. Or they can choose an entirely different and ineffective direction and feel angry or bitter. Some people who self-select out will also self-perceive that the process was somehow unfair or mean or that we are just too dumb or dense to grasp how great they are. People in that state of mind cause me to remember the singing contests on television where tone-deaf contestants insist that they are great singers and that the judges are the ones who are tone deaf. Such self-delusion is ineffective and it inhibits progress.

Here is the template I use to identify and attract viable candidates. When attracting A-level candidates, I begin with a brief, written overview of the problem, crisis, opportunity, or project. In this case I emailed the following overview to my database of fiduciaries, CPAs, fiduciary lawyers, financial executives, investment managers, advisors, and consultants:

Dear _____,

Recently I was approached by a qualified retirement plan committee chairperson for a mid-sized municipality. When he was approached with the offer to be on the committee, he was not adequately informed of the fiduciary risk he would be personally accepting. Over the years he served on the committee nobody adequately informed him of his personal risk. Eventually he was promoted to the position of committee chairperson. Once in that position, his eyes were opened to the risk he had unknowingly accepted. He believes that (much like himself) tens of thousands of committee members (as well as business owners and board of director members) are suffering emotional distress about the very real risk associated with their involvement with qualified retirement plans.

I have been asked to help him (and tens of thousands like him) to find a risk reduction solution that would also benefit the plan participants. I am reaching out to you to see if you or anyone you respect has an effective solution. Please send me an email and/or call my office to arrange a time for us to speak about any solutions you might have or know about.

Best regards,

BRW

Once this "request" was emailed to professionals with relevant expertise regarding qualified retirement plans, their risk management and performance standards, all we had to do was review and sort out the responses. We also emailed our request to a large number of stockbrokers, financial consultants, and advisors that might have relevant connections that could know of a solution if they did not personally provide one. This process of attracting, sorting, prioritizing, and then interviewing candidates required over 200 hours of my time personally. Like most entrepreneurs, I had learned long ago that sometimes the creation of new business and revenue channels requires a sufficient amount of wisely-invested time and, in this case, also a personal financial investment.

During the interview process, I not only spoke with professionals who serve, sell or manage qualified retirement plans; I also spoke with several plan providers and committee members. In so doing, I confirmed what Dale had said about how anxious and overwhelmed people are about their exposure to risk. Lots of people commented on the psychobabble sales scripts designed to "help them feel better" about the risk even though nobody was doing anything tangible to reduce the risk that was causing their anxiety.

Immediately my colleagues and I recognized that exposing this all too common practice of psychobabble coercion could prove to be a market differentiator for higher integrity professionals. Once we found, aggregated, or created an honest-to-goodness risk reduction solution, anyone using coercion or manipulation rather than actually reducing the risk would be self-eliminating. Discerning people want and demand honest tangible solutions with no exceptions regarding qualified retirement plans. Discerning stewards, plan providers, and consumers will replace purveyors of client retention scripts with people and companies that deliver a tangible reduction in risk for plan providers and committee members while improving administrative safety for the plan participants.

Our research also revealed that the majority of underserved plans are in a state of higher risk for these reasons:

1. Many qualified retirement plans are sold by undertrained people who are also under aware of the risks and who believe that decision makers want to pay the lowest price possible for plan administration and management. Most of these salespeople have no credentials specifically related to qualified retirement plan risks or fiduciary responsibilities. Because they are operating at a low level of awareness, they are unaware of the risks. That is why or how honest high integrity salespeople often fail to adequately explain the risks or the responsibilities associated with the plans they sell or service.

Just as the cream rises to the top, willing professionals, companies, and consumers can elevate beyond current conditions into greater safety and well-earned peace of mind.

2. Many stewards, including qualified retirement plan providers and committee members, are victims of their personal programming or beliefs about financial matters and spending money. Most of us were taught by parents, teachers, college professors, continuing education programs, books, etcetera, that we must conserve costs in all of our financial dealings. Unfortunately for many people, too many plan providers and committee members mistakenly believe this perception applies to fiduciary matters. Most stewards assume that good stewardship is demonstrated by proving that expenses were minimized even though such is not the case in many fiduciary matters. The wisest stewards of qualified retirement plans choose to exercise every relevant and prudent means for reducing risk and increasing safety for the plan and its participants even when such measures come at a slightly higher cost to the plan and its participants.

3. Fiduciaries of qualified retirement plans at the committee level tend to perceive their responsibilities as part time and an intrusion or distraction that interferes with their full time jobs. They are undertrained and ill equipped for the tasks at hand in this immensely complex area of financial acumen.

Yes, to a very large degree, the salespeople are selling exactly what they have been trained to sell. They are selling what they think their clients want… low cost plans. This is because some clients, including plan providers and committee members or stewards, believe they should only contract with very large or low-cost providers. Like with a lot of topics, the conundrum and the solution seemed unsolvable to many of those immersed in it. As an outsider, with a rare awareness of fiduciary matters, I quickly found, recognized, aggregated, and created solutions that have the power to improve circumstances and peace of mind for every willing person and company involved with qualified retirement plans. This is true whether the person or company involved is a professional administrator, asset manager, RIA fiduciary, a plan provider, committee member, fiduciary, or a person depending on the retirement plan proceeds for their financial independence.

In effect, my colleagues and I quickly figured out how to transcend the status quo. We established new and higher standards that automatically antiquate everyone and every company immersed in the status quo. This allows willing people to rise above and beyond current risky conditions and align with greater peace of mind.

Sometimes transcendence is achieved by observing and taking action on what seems obvious, but isn't to many other people. The next chapter will reveal a unique business channel or model that needed to be created by someone in order to fully solve the problems faced by qualified retirement plan providers and those who count on them for retirement income. Remember this case study is also a metaphor for your business if you will allow it to be. The principles contained herein are universally applicable in your business and your niche.

Chapter Eighteen

Build a Resonant Relevant Offering and the Right People Will Be Attracted to It

In the movie "Field of Dreams" the writer penned this famous quote, "If you build it he will come." Highly pragmatic people tend to view that statement as wishful thinking at best. Highly metaphysical or spiritual people tend to respond to that quote by saying something to the effect of, "Yes, that's exactly how it is supposed to work." As with a lot of topics, I think it's smart to adopt a philosophy and action plan that effectively balances pragmatic with metaphysical and spiritual perceptions. So I prefer this balanced version of the construct: Build a blatantly resonant relevant offering and the right people will be attracted to it if they know about it. It's up to you to help as many people as possible to know about it. On the flip side, those who don't resonate with your offering will be indifferent or perhaps repelled by it and that's perfectly fine.

Since my new endeavor did not turn out to be as big of a stretch outside my comfort zone and decades-old existing business model as it first appeared to be, I didn't have to create a new company or 'imagine' a new business model. I only had to add a new tab to my website entitled "Stewardship" and then make this book and my website visible to plan providers, fiduciaries, and financial services professionals who seek to be in compliance with fiduciary due diligence and conduct. Even when this book was in its earliest draft form it was effective at awakening and attracting those at risk on fiduciary matters. It also attracted people and companies that were already well suited to become next generation relevant players and innovative market leaders.

In its earliest draft form this book also attracted A-level fiduciaries who wanted to partner with me. These people already had the essential credentials, experience, and gravitas; they simply were not very skilled at self-promotion. In addition, some of them were not quite as compelling, resonant, or influential as necessary to attract the volume of opportunities they desired. They realized they could benefit from my writing and influence and together we could set a new standard.

By gathering them under one clearly-stated, compelling, blatantly resonant purpose and applying our writing and speaking skills, we have aligned them with mature-minded, highly motivated and sincere clients. This also enabled all of us to introduce the new higher standards and enhance the value, purpose, and necessity of fiduciaries.

These new standards are attractive to everyone who is serious about transcending risk, improving safety, elevating administrative effectiveness, and earning their way into a well-founded, peaceful state of mind. But be careful not to limit yourself by thinking this only applies to qualified

The Bible teaches, "Cast thy bread upon the waters ... " (Ecclesiastes 11:1). If you aspire to be a thought leader or market leader, you need to apply that principle of sharing your message (bread). If you don't have a dynamic, viral capable message (bread), you must either create your own (bake your own bread) or buy what you need from someone who can provide one (bread from a bakery).

retirement plans in the U.S.A. This new construct for fiduciary responsibility and conduct (that Macro Strategic Design, Inc. has been using for decades) can be applied in any market, anywhere in the world.

Before entering the qualified retirement plan consulting niche, I immediately recognized this reality:

1. The fiduciaries I respect and trust the most tend to be too humble to effectively market themselves, their companies or their off rings.

2. Most fiduciaries are not brilliant presenters and they often have difficulty distilling complex constructs and rules into understandable and easy to act upon points of implementation. Because of this, they often lose to well-polished salespeople who are more talented and better trained at selling the sizzle and downplaying risk and responsibility, but are also frequently less professionally competent than authentic fiduciaries.

3. Many fiduciaries are brilliant with numbers, logistics, cognitive reasoning and analytics. But those topics are uninteresting to most plan providers who view such details as distractions from their core businesses. Our transcendent standard setting model frees business leaders from the distraction elements so they can focus on optimizing income, value, and market leadership.

4. Many fiduciaries are frustrated by salespeople who under disclose complications and risk, then demand that the fiduciary support what is over sold or exaggerated by salespeople. This is a common condition in large full-service financial firms that tend to view fiduciary channels as loss leaders.

As an author, speaker, mentor, and trainer, I knew that I could help those at risk, such as plan providers, committee members, and board members, quickly come to clarity about the pending catastrophe that awaits them if they do not take immediate action to correct their situations. I could expose the under disclosure, coercion, and manipulation that runs rampant. I knew I could elevate the awareness of those who are underrepresented and over sold. I was confident that I could expose how companies and salespeople run away from personal or corporate responsibility by refusing to accept the standard of care that obligates them to understand, articulate in writing, and protect the clients' best interests. At the same time, I urge all service providers, vendors, and advisors to elevate themselves into market leadership by embracing this new and higher standard of stewardship responsibility from which most salespeople are running away.

Discerning people prefer to do business with people in every field who have the courage and conviction to stand behind their advice, products, and the results that follow. Discerning people prefer transparency, honesty, and accountability from providers in every niche. People and companies that want to earn the trust, hearts, and minds of discerning buyers, investors, voters, donors, vendors, allies, or friends need to move themselves into alignment with being trustworthy, transparent, honest, and accountable. People who are separated from market leadership in discerning markets would be wise to elevate into a higher integrity business model and behaviors. Knowing where you are in alignment, where you are out of alignment, and what to do about it, is crucial to your success.

As voters, donors, investors, and consumers awaken into greater discernment, they begin to discover where and how they have been underrepresented. They begin to recognize sales schemes, coercion, spin, and manipulation and they let

As you let go of defensive status quo thinking and behavior you can elevate into transcendent thinking and being.

---

go of those relationships. They elevate into new relationships where they are fully respected, honored, and served. Those who are capable of elevating their business models, practices, deliverables, and results can use this construct which renders competitors irrelevant or obsolete without being combative or directly saying anything negative about the competition or the status quo. In theory, this could even work for high integrity politicians who sufficiently apply themselves to a transcendent way of being.

For myself and many people moving away from a combative or competitive view of business modeling into transcendent ways of being is sometimes difficult, and even painful. Once I figured out how to do this for myself, I began helping other willing people in a variety of business niches. The more I did so, the easier it became for me to teach, mentor, and support clients. The more transcendent thinking you are willing to put yourself through, the easier it becomes. Transcendent thinking can lead to transcendent business models, platforms, market attraction programs, and ways of doing and being. However, that is only true to the degree that we are willing to let go of or to outgrow the status quo before it devours our hopes and dreams for the future … and us.

Part of what I have learned about transcendence is this:

Transcendent thinking, constructs, and behavior are usually just about as easy or as hard as we make them. If we perceive this will be painful, impossible, or very hard, it most likely will be that way. If we allow ourselves to accept the belief that transcendence will be easy, natural, and flowing for us, it often will be that way. Transcendence is always as available to us as we are to it. For every step towards or into transcendence we take, transcendence will move at least one or more steps closer towards or into us. Sometimes transcendence will embrace us and take us for a quantum leap if we are sufficiently willing to allow that to happen.

You might find out, as I did, that you already have a business model that can easily add another revenue channel or two in a way that is seamless, feels natural and effortless to you and to discerning consumers. For people, businesses, charities, and other organizations that are already philosophically aligned with this construct, the journey into alignment will be shorter, faster and easier than it will be for those who misread this as a new selling proposition or manipulation scheme. For some of us, this is our way of being. For others it will be yet another trend they want to exploit for profit at the expense of the naïve and powerless. I trust that my writing, speaking, and other offerings, the bread I've cast upon the waters, will be found by people who want to discern and elevate themselves away from the scammers and imposters.

Chapter Nineteen

Imposters and Wannabes

Several years ago I was being interviewed for a magazine by a writer that was obviously underprepared. About five minutes into that interview I was explaining how transcendent ideas and methods positively affect and elevate our clients and the advisors that support their progress. Somewhat surprisingly he interrupted me and asked if I had heard of a man named Lance Flatue (name changed to protect identity). I told him that I was familiar with Mr. Flatue. The journalist then asked me if I was familiar with the word plagiarism. I responded, "Of course I am."

Journalist: The ideas and methods you have been describing are remarkably close to Mr. Flatue's offerings aren't they?

Me: Yes, they certainly seem to be quite similar. What is your point?

Journalist: Well, to be blunt, Mr. Flatue is a friend of mine and I don't appreciate you plagiarizing his work and taking credit as the inventor.

Me: Why do you believe that I'm the plagiarist and that Flatue is the creator?

Journalist: Because I know that Mr. Flatue is a man of the highest integrity and that he is dedicated to helping as many people as possible before he dies of cancer. Perhaps you don't know that my friend has terminal cancer and every dime you make while pretending to be the creator of these ideas and methods is being stolen right out of his pocket when he really needs every dime he can get to prolong his life and ease his suffering. You are the reason that his widow and children will be penniless when he dies!

That interview was not going the way I had expected it to. I was used to being treated with a lot more respect. This was the first time in my life that I had been accused of stealing Macro Strategic Planning® or any of its derivatives. Here is how I responded:

Me: I can see that you are very passionate about protecting your friend. I have heard from several people that Mr. Flatue is very likable and seems to be honest. Yes I am aware that he has terminal cancer.

Journalist: This is even worse than I thought. You know all of that and still you are stealing his ideas and claiming to be the inventor of all of this.

Me: Yes, I am the inventor, creator and person who established all of these ideas and methods we have been discussing. Unfortunately for Mr. Flatue and his admirers I invented them, field tested them, and perfected them; then paid for and received trademarks, service marks, and copyrights on them back when Mr. Flatue was still in college.

Journalist: So you are claiming that you have the trademarks, patents, etcetera?

Me: My lawyers have sent Mr. Flatue more than one cease-and-desist letter. We planned on suing him for trademark and copyright infringements, but once we learned that he was dying from untreatable pancreatic cancer, we decided not to pursue that path.

Journalist: It's hard for me to accept what you are saying is true. You expect me to believe you over my friend? A man I am certain is good and honest?

Me: May I suggest that, as a journalist, it is your obligation to find the truth and report it? I've heard that Mr. Flatue is quite charismatic, engaging and very likable. Lots of people think he's a genius and trustworthy.

Journalist: Well one of you is deceiving a lot of people. One of you is a plagiarist.

Me: I'll send you my lawyer's contact information. He will get you all of the copyright, trademark, service mark, and other details that prove beyond any reasonable doubt that I am the creator and the one who established and proved the value of these concepts.

Journalist: Thank you. I will follow-up on this then perhaps we can schedule a new interview.

That concluded our interview. That journalist did not follow-up with my lawyer. My lawyer followed up with him, but he did not contact me for another interview. We did not see any article related to any of this in his magazine. All moderately successful con artists are likable. They are charismatic and seem to be trustworthy. They have to be. All successful con artists, imposters, or plagiarists depend upon people failing to perform a reasonable level of due diligence. They are gifted liars and they know how to tell you the lies you would most like to hear. Your willingness to believe in them without due diligence and verification of claims is essential to their success. Most journalists are not trained to perform fiduciary level due diligence and that condition is the root of a lot of avoidable suffering and embarrassment. As you move forward into mastery at thought leadership and market prominence, you must protect your creations with full documentation, trademarks, service marks, copyrights, or patents. If you do not, you are actively inviting thieves to claim ownership of your life's work.

Human beings tend to be resentful when their beliefs are proven to be misguided or false. We do not like to learn that we have been duped or that we have misplaced our trust, our money, or our reputations with a deceitful person, cause or enterprise. The less mature we are, the more likely we are to blame the messenger of truth. The more we love the lie or the liar, the more difficult it is for us to correct our thinking or our actions and direction.

As we allow ourselves to mature our minds and develop our mastery over our emotions, we are more likely to let go of our attachment to false beliefs and the people that have misled us. Did you know that even after famous con artists and Ponzi schemers are sent to prison, many of those from whom they stole still refuse to believe that the convict is guilty? Yes, their money is obviously gone and they will never get that money back. But in spite of this reality, they cannot allow themselves to believe they were wrong about the convicted and obviously guilty person.

The more mature the mind, the easier it is to let go of harmful or ineffective people, ideas, and constructs and the harder it is to be taken in by them. The more mature our minds become, the easier it is to let go of the status quo and the people who tenaciously protect it. A mature-minded person always performs significant due diligence and does not rush to judgment. Mature-minded people are less likely to mistake criminals for heroes. Mature-minded people are less likely to be duped by fraudulent scientists, politicians, psychologists, investment gurus, false messiahs, quacks, and disingenuous

All successful con artists, imposters, or plagiarists depend upon people failing to perform a reasonable level of due diligence. They are gifted liars and they know how to tell you the lies you would most like to hear. As W.C. Fields so famously said, "There's a sucker born every minute."

Always perform an exceptional level of due diligence so you won't be one.

lovers. Mature-minded people are more likely to accept and benefit from shifts in financial markets, culture, religion, or spirituality.

Some people love imposters more than they can bring themselves to love originators. Some have no misgivings about wearing rip-off copies of fine jewelry or clothing. Some people will knowingly pay an imposter to give a speech, chisel a sculpture, paint a picture, or act as their guide in order to save some money — unaware of the damage and ripple effect they are causing. Doing the right thing even when you are certain no one is watching can be hard sometimes, but it is the best path for less regret and greater self-respect.

For the past few decades we have been helping Fortune 500 and smaller companies train their executives, sales-people, consultants, and advisors. In one of these Fortune 500 cases we began with a pilot program that would launch their Platinum Services division. We began with fifty of their smartest, boldest, well-proven producers, otherwise known as salespeople. Of course their actual business titles were not Producer or Salesperson. The official title given them was Financial Management Consultant (I have altered that title a bit to protect people from embarrassment).

The pilot program was hugely successful. That group of people accomplished the following within 120 days of the training:

- Each participant attracted at least $25 million in new assets under management

- Reduced work week to 35 hours or less

- Improved life balance

- Improved relationships with every family member that wanted to enjoy a better relationship

- Elevated effectiveness and trust with existing clients, allies, vendors, and referral sources

Well before the 120-day trial period was completed, that company offered us a contract to help them identify and elevate 1,000 of their advisors into the Platinum Services program. Everyone was optimistic and we had a lot of positive energy to make this happen. However, there were several status quo lovers and protectors that resisted what we were teaching and doing — even though the status quo had a very long track record for being completely unattractive to the types of discerning and affluent clientele they were hoping to connect with. The success of the pilot program, and my company's rich history of success in that high-level client market, meant nothing to the status quo protectors.

Both the pilot roll-out and the launch of the second-wave of trainees were massively successful in the same ways described above. But status quo addicts, a.k.a. those who are dysfunctionally attached to the status quo, generally believe that it is their responsibility to get in the way of new ideas that are disruptive to the current way of being. They must find fault. In this case the big complaint was this:

> The content is too advanced for some of our people, so we (meaning me) must simplify until everyone can succeed in that program.

Please remember, this Platinum Services program was designed to attract, connect with, and engage only discerning affluent people. This platform was intentionally not intended for the masses or the type of advisors who play at that undiscerning market level. Simply stated; discerning people demand levels of attention and support that average people, including some advisors, cannot understand or deliver. The Platinum Services program was not supposed to be easy for ordinary advisors to understand or to succeed with. In fact, there is no such thing as an advanced or elite program wherein every professional that enrolls can or will succeed. Therefore the request for simplification to the point where each advisor was guaranteed success was destined to guarantee the failure of the program.

In a private one-on-one call with the President of that company, I pointed out that fact. I explained that advanced constructs and methods such as neurosurgery, rocket science, quantum physics, and supporting discerning affluent people cannot be dumbed down to the point where ordinary people can excel as professionals. By their very nature of complexity, those fields are above and beyond the intellectual reach and behavioral capacity of ordinary people. For the most part, those fields of endeavor tend to be repellent to ordinary people. Elite programs are exclusively suitable for people who are talented and dedicated enough to make themselves exceptional.

We agreed that I would simplify as much as I deemed reasonable so that more people could understand and succeed, provided that the President strongly encouraged the students to perform all of the self-study and participate in the weekly mentoring sessions. This was not a program suited for dabblers or excuse makers.

The revised curriculum was substantially simplified, but of course the status quo defenders were not satisfied. Those defenders either could not or would not understand the fundamental truth that some people cannot excel with advanced or elite constructs or subject matter. Some people lack the work ethic, or the IQ or EQ, to become excellent or masterful at neurosurgery, rocket science, law, taxation, or macro or micro strategic thinking and planning. Because the Platinum Services platform was intended only for elite customers and clients and elite professionals, it would not succeed if staffed by ordinary people who want to imagine they are elite professionals even though they're not.

Eventually I refused to further dumb down my training to the lowest common denominator. I warned the President that her Platinum Services program was going to be neutered by people who love the status quo, their comfort, and egos more than they love being masterful in an elite market niche. When our contract was up, I lovingly let go of that relationship. I politely refused to submit another contract. I even sat in on my replacement's first presentation. I could immediately see why they had chosen him and his platform. He was somewhat of a disciple of my methods for languaging and thought leadership. Important for the delusional lovers of the status quo, he believed that market leadership was all about conversations relating to holistic Macro Strategic Planning®. My deep conviction is that mastery goes way beyond conversations and deeply into the dynamic execution of all of the relevant and timely details.

Once my firm was out of the way, the status quo defenders and their Bruce Wright sound alike created a booklet and advertising campaign to attract discerning affluent consumers. None of them met the sophisticated expectations of those consumers. It failed in part because it lacked authenticity. Any decent high school-level actor can practice his way into sounding like me when introducing 100-1,000 Year Micro and Macro Strategic Planning™. They can mimic my words and even act as though they possess my conviction, passion, and expertise. But when it comes right down to it, discerning people want something far beyond engaging phrases, interesting ideas, and cool conversations. These kinds of people demand tangible deliverables, appropriate actions, and measurable extraordinary results — and they know how to spot it when it's there and when it's not.

Their dumbed down life-planning booklet and platform

destroyed the upward momentum we had established because the target audience of consumers and advisors recognized that it was an overly simplistic gadget or selling scheme that lacked real power and authenticity. Discerning buyers, customers, clients, voters, and donors prefer to surround themselves with and trust their future success with masterful dedicated professionals rather than wannabes, dabblers, imposters, yes people, and status quo defenders. You can save yourself time by accepting these truths as they are written or spoken here or you can go the long route and learn them the hard, expensive or painful way through your own trials and errors. Your choice.

Provable excellence matters. Extraordinary results are rarely if ever available through people who choose to apply dumbed down modalities or take shortcuts to success. Authenticity is detectable and eventually it is fully revealed in outcomes.

Chapter Twenty

Aligning, Attracting and Engaging for Transcendence

I love to watch documentaries and television shows about nature, animals, and surviving in various wilderness areas of the world. This began for me when I was a young boy and over the years I have learned a great deal about nature, animals, and the human ability to learn, adapt, grow, overcome adversity, and succeed. I remember one program where the television star and his camera crew were surviving in a dense tropical rainforest with a small band of natives. The television star went into detail about how difficult it was to find food or potable water. He complained about the biting and stinging insects, scorpions, spiders, and venomous snakes.

What I noticed was how easy it was in the jungle for the natives. While the "civilized" people were struggling, the "uncivilized" natives were easily going about their normal life and thriving in the flow of nature. In one scene, the star was freaking out over a giant tarantula that had walked casually into their camp. The star and his crew watched and filmed in amazement as one of the natives very easily and gently captured the spider with his bare hands then calmly and routinely killed it. He then roasted that spider over the fire. As the spider was cooking, the native skillfully used a stick to scrape off the spider's body hair as it is hazardous for humans to eat that hair. Then the native offered some freshly cooked spider meat to the star and his crew. Most of them chose not to eat the spider meat even though they were hungry. Apparently one man's menace can be another man's food.

Civilized people get lost and die in the wilderness every year in places where "less civilized" or "uncivilized" natives thrive in the flow of nature. This occurs in barren deserts, tropical jungles, remote islands, and arctic tundra. What seems desolate and inhospitable to some is often the home of others who thrive there. If you refuse to recognize easily obtainable seaweed, crabs, or shellfish as food, you could starve to death while surrounded by tons of edible things. Plant life, insects, reptiles, shellfish, scorpions, and spiders can be food if you are sufficiently open to recognizing them as such and are willing to eat them.

Just about every day, at least one or more people ask me to help them overcome some challenge or to transcend their competition. On one of these occasions, the president of a trust company called me and said, "Bruce, our people need more 'at bats' with wealthy, discerning consumers. We have the best people in the industry and we have the best platform to help customers, we just cannot get in front of enough qualified prospects. Can you help us?"

Having had this type of conversation with many business leaders in a variety of fields of endeavor numerous times, I was able to take that man through a series of important questions. That conversation was so familiar to me and the questioning and self-discovery process so universally relevant, that it could flow naturally even while driving in rush hour traffic in Los Angeles.

As this leader proceeded to answer each question with absolute honesty, our conversation helped him self-discover several crucial truths including:

1. His people were not demonstrably superior to their competitors. In fact, his people were interchangeable with those of his competitors.

2. His platform was so similar to his competitors that it was perceived to be the same as all of the B-A level offerings in the marketplace.

3. Not enough at bats is a symptom, it's not the problem. It's the predictable result when a professional or enterprise is insufficiently relevant, resonant, unique, impactful, or valued as a thought leader.

This next part was the hardest truth for him to accept:

Holding a one-day training retreat would not be enough to overcome their circumstances. Their way of being was producing their results and lack of what they wanted. To move from lack or scarcity into abundance and attraction, they would have to elevate and realign their way of being.

Many consultants, advisors, coaches, mentors, and teachers would have us believe that one day with them and a $100,000 fee is all that is necessary to overcome the problem of not getting enough at bats. The inconvenient truth however is this:

> To increase your "at bats" you must elevate into a new way of being. Your messaging, business model, marketing, and deliverables need to be blatantly relevant, resonant and impactful. Who you are and the way you behave screams so loudly that it drowns out even the most expensive advertising campaign. Be who and what you claim to be. Aspire to be and become what matters to your clients and you will solve your "at bats" dilemma.

Until a professional or an enterprise becomes sufficiently resonant, relevant, and compelling as a thought leader, it will struggle to connect with clients, customers, donors, or voters. Especially if you want more discerning affluent clients. It is up to each of us to move ourselves into sufficient alignment with the people with whom we want to connect. Just as there is no such thing as a one-day course that will grow a white belt into being a masterful black belt, no one-day course will solve a too-few-at-bats condition.

Elevating that leader's people, platform, and offerings into relevant, resonant, compelling thought leadership would only be possible if they sufficiently invested the necessary energy, focus, and millions of dollars of financial resources to become what their market needs someone to be. All of this would take much more than a one-day training retreat and $100,000.

Shifting out of the "not enough at bats" condition into an abundant state of being condition where you are sufficiently attractive, relevant, compelling, and resonant is accomplished through acquisition of the right kinds of IP, patents, trademarks, etcetera or your own growth via research and development. You can find the kind of money necessary to fund the shift through your merger and acquisition or research and development budgets. Or you can raise the capital necessary to fund your growth and ascension into thought and market leadership. Then you will have to elevate the training and marketing aspects of your business. There are no shortcuts, quick tips, or cheap strategies to actually shift and elevate your way of being. Anyone who tells you otherwise is either insufficiently wise or they are about to sell you on their own "Stone Soup" scheme, a concept that will be introduced in Chapter 23.

As you might expect this far into this book, some leaders are willing to lead their people and their organizations out of the ordinary and into being extraordinary. In this particular case, that leader was insufficiently willing to solve the core problems and actually grow into who and what the market needs someone to be. It was expedient for him to choose a motivational speaker that could fire up his people. He actually believed that external motivational jibber jabber and walking barefoot across hot coals would transform his people and his enterprise.

Within a year that man had been replaced because of disappointing performance. But, he was replaced by a woman who seems to possess a carbon copy of her predecessor's mind. Of course, they still do not have enough at bats. Their people learned how to walk barefoot on hot coals and use a martial arts technique to break ¼ inch pine boards with their fists. Unfortunately for them, discerning affluent people do not consider those newly acquired skill sets to be relevant, resonant, or sufficiently valuable to feel attracted to that trust company, its people, or any of its offerings.

Instead of struggling to find new clients, wouldn't it be a more enjoyable business experience to attract them effortlessly?

Rather than begging for referrals, wouldn't you prefer to attract them organically without asking for them?

Wouldn't it be nice if you could easily awaken your desired clientele to realize that you have more personally relevant and valuable offerings than your competitors?

These are a few of the questions I like to ask leaders who want to increase opportunity flow or at bats. Nearly all of them answer these questions similarly to how you answered them. However, only the greatest leaders will actually do what must be done in order to move their people and their enterprises into the thought leadership and market leadership

Are you a manager or a leader? Leaders can transcend to an elevated way of being. Managers maintain and oversee the status quo.

position. The majority of leaders are not capable of such transcendence because at heart they are managers who are adept at overseeing the status quo. This means that nearly all of your competitors will still be struggling with the same deficiencies five years from now.

> Managers tend to protect and serve the status quo while leaders are constantly aligning themselves with new ideas, people, and constructs that transcend what is available now.

Sometimes, perhaps even at this very moment, the answer you are seeking will be right in front of you. You could even be holding it in your hands, looking at it or listening to it and still not realize that the answer you need is immediately available to you. The great song writer, singer, and musician Paul Simon wrote, "Still a man hears what he wants to hear and disregards the rest." Because all human beings are susceptible to this phenomenon, we must consistently remind ourselves of this simple truth:

> What you are seeking is waiting for you to discover "It." That special "It" can be a transcendent idea, business construct, client magnet, ally, guide, or mentor. It can be a melody, phrase, lyric, or punch line. Whatever "It" is that you are seeking already is. It already exists. However, you might have to get beyond the belief that you must be the originator or creator of "It" if you are to get where you desire to be next with the speed and ease desired.

The big question for human beings that want to elevate themselves, their relationships, their circumstances, or their enterprises is this:

Are you sufficiently willing to recognize, hear, see and accept "It" right now, even if you are not the originator, creator, or owner of the solution you need now to get to where you want to be next?

When you are not sufficiently willing to receive or accept "It," you will not recognize "It" even when "It" is available to you, perhaps being held in your hands or coming into your ears right now. Another way of explaining this phenomenon is as follows:

As soon as you begin to move yourself into *alignment* with what you want, you make yourself available to "It." The more available you become to "It," the more available "It" becomes to you.

Yes, this is fundamental Law of Alignment awareness. But what many people fail to grasp is this:

The Law of Alignment activates and puts into motion the Law of Attraction.

No human being can attract a good thing or relationship that he or she is not available to, ready for, and sufficiently willing to accept. In other words, even if you are starving to death but you are unwilling to eat a tarantula, you will not consider the tarantula to be food. Starving to death even when food is available happens to people every day on a meta-phorical or metaphysical basis. Sometimes it literally happens to people. This is all about willingness, readiness, adaptability, flexibility, and brain elasticity or plasticity.

The strategic allies, joint venture partners, clients, advisors, mentors, financial capital, and leadership position you want next are all waiting for you to put yourself into the degree of

> **"Sometimes when you innovate, you make mistakes. It is best to admit them quickly, and get on with improving your other innovations.** —*Steve Jobs*

alignment necessary for you to recognize and accept them. This demands some initiative on your part. The inertia begins with you and if momentum is to be sustained, you are the one responsible for sustaining it. Yes, you can hire and trust certain people to help with this, but as the leader, inertia and momentum are up to you.

Some proactive behavior on your part is necessary because honorable people operating on the level(s) above your awareness only want to collaborate with people functioning at their level or higher. They are not looking for people at lower levels of consciousness or readiness because those people are not sufficiently ready or willing to be or do what must be done to accomplish the desired outcomes on the higher level. We seldom get bigger, stronger, wiser, or more effective by dragging, coercing, manipulating, or forcing unready and unwilling people up the stairs with us.

Try thinking about it this way:

Imagine that you are striving to be at the next level, someplace higher, above and beyond where you and your competitors are today. Imagine that you are on the sixth floor of a building. You cannot see how many floors there really are, but according to the buttons in the elevator there are ten floors above ground and several underground levels for parking.

> Being on the sixth floor, would you want to invest the time, energy, and cost of business to travel down to the basement and get some unready or insufficiently

> **Ripple in still water when there is no pebble tossed nor wind to blow.** —*Jerry Garcia*
>
> *Be the ripple no known entities make.*

prepared people and carry them up to the sixth floor and put them into positions of responsibility? Do world-class chess masters get to be masterful by playing against people below their ability? Of course not. To get better at chess or business you must be good enough to intrigue or entice people who are more advanced than you, or on a floor above you, to play with you. In business you do that by paying them in either cash or equity or a combination of both. In chess you enter tournaments and earn your way to play against better opponents by winning the preliminary matches. You can either earn or pay for the attention of those who operate above your current consciousness and skill level.

Some people will not do what is necessary to elevate out of the basement. Others will be content to spend their entire lives living on the sixth floor even if they are miserable there. Some will constantly elevate themselves with the penthouse being their goal. Some of us realize that there is no limit to the number of possibilities and opportunities available to us.

Some of us realize that we can attract, purchase, rent or earn the attention of those who exist and comfortably operate on the floor(s) above where we are now. Allowing oneself to be limited by so-called IQ or EQ can be a choice. Rarely does it have to be or remain our limiting reality.

The best or most effective leaders of today and tomorrow refuse to allow themselves to be mere managers of the status

> **"It is the greatest shot of adrenaline to be doing what you have wanted to do so badly. You almost feel like you could fly without the plane.** —*Charles Lindbergh*

quo and its conditions such as not enough at bats. The most effective leaders constantly strive to remove or transcend the obstacles that impede the success of their people or their enterprise. Great leaders refuse to be hampered by an operating system or way of being that results in not enough at bats.

We live amongst an abundance of resources, talented people, masterful people, and unlimited possibilities. You may not be able to muster enough money from your training budget to obtain the people, platform or solution you need next. However, that money is either already in your firm's acquisition budget, your research and development budget, or your slush fund. Or it can be raised from strategic allies or vendors. Or it can be raised as debt or capital through investors or hedge funds or venture capital funds, etcetera. The world is a much smaller place when you view it merely through your own budget or checkbook. As soon as you decide to step into your greatness, you will recognize ways to tap into and connect with abundance that transcends your prior perspectives and limitations.

When you allow yourself to combine the Rate Your Awareness & Expertise exercise found in chapter nine with the ten floor building metaphor in this chapter, a whole new perspective becomes available to you. All mentally and emotionally healthy people can improve their awareness and expertise by studying, focusing on, being mentored, and applying themselves fully up to a new level. Now this is where we get metaphysical:

On the roof, it's peaceful as can be, and there the world below won't bother me... Look at the city here you just have to wish to make it so. — *Carole King*

Once a person arrives on the roof of the building, she begins to become aware of additional buildings and bridges that allow travel between multiple buildings. Every truly masterful person I have ever met perceives himself or herself to be a perpetual student. This is because mastery of one thing leads human beings to awareness of other things wherein we are novices. Ascension exposes us to nooks and crannies or nuances previously invisible to us because we used to be unable to see them. Mastery requires a letting go of ego, which automatically opens us to new possibilities that transcend current awareness, vision or sense of certainty. Moving from building to building reveals treasure troves of new possibilities and topics for us to learn about and to profit from. Once you ascend your existing building, you will become aware of other taller buildings awaiting your exploration and ascension.

People stuck in ego or convinced that they know everything have not reached the roof of the building they are currently in. They are unaware of the other buildings or of their importance. They are like the blind man that is certain he is experiencing a large powerful snake — unable or unwilling to comprehend that he is touching the trunk of an elephant. Advisors and their clients get stuck like this when they think and behave in a transactional rather than a holistic way. I have seen lots of successful real estate, stock or merger transactions wherein little or no attention was paid to macro consequences, and millions of dollars in avoidable taxes were lost. Perhaps worse than that, I have met many a seller who was miserable post transaction because insufficient attention was invested in understanding how to envision and manifest a balanced, significant, and joyful life after the sale of the business. Who, what, and where you want to be next needs to be the driving vision for how sales or mergers are structured. Having a lot of cash while lacking clarity of your purpose and highest self can be dangerous.

The more time and resources we put into elevating our holistic awareness and behavior, the more synchronicity we experience or create. Transaction-minded people or narrowly focused people cannot comprehend all of the essential components for establishing and sustaining thought or market leadership. They only understand their piece of the elephant. Usually because that one piece of the elephant is how they get paid or because it represents their role in this world. Perhaps they perceive that piece of the elephant to represent their very identity and purpose. Oftentimes this is because that is all their minds are capable of understanding. However, far too many people are self-limiting in that respect. The necessary IQ and EQ often already exist, although they do not access the gifts they possess but have yet to experience and express. Some people are brilliant at one piece of the elephant and they connect their identity and whole sense of self to that one thing at which they are recognized at being brilliant. Then one day that thing ceases to exist or it becomes irrelevant. If you are the most respected tax lawyer in Chicago and the income tax system gets simplified into a value added or flat tax system, your piece of the elephant and your identity will have been redefined. Whether you are ready and willing or not, change is coming.

I encourage you to elevate yourself to the roof of the building and encourage you to do so as politely and lovingly as possible. Don't allow anyone or anything to get in your way. On the roof, you can see not only the entire elephant, you will be able to see people, possibilities, and treasure troves of unexplored opportunities waiting for someone like you to recognize them, express them, and give life to them. The status quo is like an elevator that stops on floor six or seven. To elevate beyond that level, you will have to power your own way floor by floor to the top. Let go of your restraints and move up to the roof of the building. Lots of amazing people and ideas are right there waiting for you right now.

Chapter Twenty-One

Coercion, Rudeware, Greed, and Unwise Policies are Not Part of the Recipe for Market Leadership

Like many people experiencing this book, I use a smartphone just about every day. My latest one was acquired at a store that only sells its own cellular service. Let's call that company Bebloaten. At least for a day or two my new phone was one of the most state of the art devices. I was told that it would take no time to get used to it because it uses the Android system I was already accustomed to using. The salesman was wrong about that. He oversold benefits that either didn't exist or were irrelevant to me and he severely downplayed the complications and other negatives.

The biggest problem has been that my phone was delivered to me with lots of irrelevant and unwanted applications and software that use up memory and battery life. Some people refer to this as "bloatware." Worst of all Bebloaten representatives assure me that none of it can be uninstalled. This irritates my sense of civility and freedom. I am a liberty-loving American and I do not appreciate having anything or anyone forced on me. Every day or two my phone indicates that some apps need to be updated. Amongst them are nearly always certain unwanted irrelevant apps. Each time this happens it feels like someone is rubbing salt into my wounded liberty-loving psyche.

Rudeness, arrogance, and greed are the behaviors experienced here. I am perfectly capable of finding and choosing what apps or software I want or need. The more crap apps I find being forced on me, the more I want to change providers. My phone's manufacturer keeps asking me for permission to share all of my data and preferences with whomever they want to share it with. I cannot find any way to eliminate their program called "home sense" or unsubscribe from it or uninstall it. Bebloaten tells me that there is nothing I can do about it. I beg to differ.

When the phone manufacturer, Bebloaten, NFL Mobile, and Kids Mode, etcetera put their respective brain trusts, which I will refer to as "the coalition," into discussions about how to optimize their exposure and profits, I believe they forgot one of the basic elements in the recipe for success. That basic element is politeness. Many of us past the age of fifty are certain that society is less polite now than it was when we were young.

The current etiquette norm seems surprisingly arrogant, assumptive, and condescending about attitudes and business models. "Rudeware," as I like to call this phenomenon, occurs when impolite, arrogant people get together and decide to force their crap apps and unwanted or so-called offerings on you that are irrelevant to you. They do not even possess enough politeness to allow you to easily and quickly opt out of what a customer judges to be a crap app.

I love watching NFL games on television or online, but I have zero use for NFL Mobile. The rude people in charge at the coalition don't want me to be able to opt out. There are no circumstances where I will allow children to play games on my phone. Nevertheless, my phone was pre-loaded with Kids Mode and I am not allowed to uninstall it. When you have a moment, please peruse the Kids Mode thread. It is full of negative comments and even some profanity from clients who hate that app. What we seem to hate the most is the fact that this irrelevant and useless app cannot be uninstalled. What we hate second most about Kids Mode is that every once in a while it insists upon being updated. More salt in the wounded psyche of those who don't like or respect the arrogance, rudeness, and condescension of purveyors of Rudeware.

This prompts a recommendation for all who create, sell, and support products and services:

> Don't think and act in rude, condescending and arrogant ways so you don't drive prospective clients directly into the arms of less offensive providers. You can save a fortune on advertising by being polite, respectful and helpful with the clients you already have and those you wish to attract in the future.

"Stupid is as stupid does." — Mama Gump

I tend to rent cars frequently. Having been profoundly disrespected by credit card companies over the years, I now choose not to use credit cards. I use debit cards. Some companies however have an incentive or a strategic alliance with banks or credit card companies and they try to coerce or push us into using credit cards instead of debit cards. Some companies are so financially ignorant that they cannot figure out that debit card payments are just as green as credit card payments. Debit cards use real money that is already available in the account.

Enter the surprisingly ridiculous policy of Centerprisal Rent-A-Car. A while ago I called Centerprisal to rent a car for a couple of days. Something I had done many times before without any complications or aggravations. Over the telephone I verified that they had a suitable car at an agreeable price and gave them my Gold Member number and debit card number to lock in the reservation. I told them I would be there at 4:00 that afternoon to pick up the car ... so far, so good. Upon arriving I gave the customer service representative my license, proof of insurance, and the debit card I had used earlier to confirm my reservation. This was the same procedure I had followed several times before with Centerprisal. Surprisingly the young man asked me if I had brought my utility bills and pay stubs necessary to rent the car. At first I thought I must be on some hidden camera television show or perhaps one of my friends had set up some kind of a practical joke. I looked around the room for any signs of a camera crew and then I asked the representative if this was a joke. He assured me that it was no joke. I inquired as to why I had not been informed of this policy when I called and made the reservation for the car earlier using that same debit card to lock it all in place. He said, "I don't know why, but that's our new policy."

There was no time to get back home and find utility bills and then get back in time to conclude the transaction before they closed. Because I am not anyone's employee, I don't have any pay stubs. Many entrepreneurs, inventors, and venture capitalists don't have pay stubs. Retired people don't have pay stubs and I don't know anyone who walks around with utility bills in their wallets. I asked that young man if he encounters very many people walking around with their utility bills and pay stubs on them. He said, "No." I informed him that self-employed people, retired people, and authors usually don't have any pay stubs. Many retired people live with their children and they don't have any utility bills in their own names. He informed me that this policy was designed to reduce car theft. He went on to say that people with credit cards have been vetted by a creditor, so they are less likely to steal cars. The fact that I did have written proof that I have been vetted by the FBI didn't sway him. In the under-aware mind of that oblivious young man, a credit card company's vetting is better than the FBI at identifying criminals and car thieves.

I cancelled my reservation and resolved to investigate that policy. Over the next couple of weeks I interviewed several customer service representatives and branch managers at various Centerprisal locations. I learned that was in fact their policy. I also learned that policy only applies to their stores located far away from airports. I asked how many miles far away was and none of them gave me a definitive answer. I also learned that their stores close to airports will accept your flight itinerary in lieu of pay stubs and utility bills. I inquired if a train or bus itinerary would suffice and I was told, "No." I called their corporate office but could not secure an interview with anyone.

So here you have a corporate policy built upon an unproven bias that people who do not have pay stubs are more likely to steal cars. The policy discriminates against retired, those unable to work, unemployed, and self-employed people. It even discriminates against multimillionaires who do not walk around with utility bills or pay stubs and prefer to use debit cards over credit cards.

Apparently the folks included in the Centerprisal brain trust could not figure any of that out. Apparently they cannot figure out that auto theft insurance is available. Obviously they are not aware of GPS tracking systems that would help them or police locate overdue or stolen cars. Centerprisal Rent-A-Car poses no threat to the existing market leader. They are not capable of thought leadership either. I told each person and manager that I interviewed that I was going to share their policy with the world. None of them was concerned about it and the company was unresponsive to my request for a written explanation. This indicated to me that Centerprisal does not want self-employed entrepreneurs, multimillionaires, unemployed disabled people, unemployed people, or retired people as customers.

Greedy Coercion

Greedy policies are recognizable very quickly. Most greedy policies have little or nothing to do with bringing or adding value to consumers. Recently I decided to pay rent on a property with cash. Something I have done before without any problem. I walked into a local branch of Chases Every Penny Bank with a couple thousand dollars in cash well below the $10,000 money-laundering threshold and the account information for the deposit. The teller informed me that Chases Every Penny Bank has a new policy. As of a few weeks ago, non-account holders cannot deposit cash into their customers' accounts.

Here it comes … But if I open up an account with them that day, they would gladly transfer the money for me, for free. I asked for the manager and politely requested that she waive that policy. At first she implied that she couldn't because of federal and state banking laws. So I said, "So this is a bank. As you can see, this is genuine U.S. currency. I know for a fact that there are zero state or federal laws that prohibit you from accepting cash deposits of $2,000.00 into any existing customer's account." At that point she rather sheepishly admitted that there were no laws against such a deposit. I asked how we could get this done right now. She responded that I could buy a money order from them for $10.00 and then they would deposit that money order into their customer's account. I understood their business model right away. That is a bank that does not like to do business with cash and it wants to charge both the payer and the receiver, their existing customer, on as many parts of transactions as possible.

A few years ago one of my friends bought a bicycle from me for a couple thousand dollars. His account was at a Chases Every Penny Bank right next door to the bank I was using at that time. I decided to just cash his check drawn on that branch. The teller informed me that if I opened up a Chases

"Don't be "penny wise and pound foolish." — *Robert Burton*

Every Penny Bank account he would cash my check for free. If I did not open an account he would have to charge me $7.50 to cash the check. Please remember that Chases Every Penny Bank was already making money off my friend but that was not enough to satiate their greed.

The choice presented was: a) Be coerced into opening an account with their bank; or b) Pay them a fee each time you do business with one of their customers. I guess that Chases Every Penny Bank is successful at coercing people into doing something they probably do not need to do or want to do.

Every year, and usually several times each year, some private banker from Chases Every Penny Bank calls me. They want me and my business as clients. They want me to introduce them to my clients. So I ask them these questions:

1. What will Chases Every Penny Bank do for me or my clients that we are not already getting from one or more of your competitors?

2. Are you willing to accept full fiduciary responsibility on any and all money we put with your bank?

3. How can I be sure that once I become your client or my clients become your clients that we will not be nickeled and dimed on charges and fees?

So far Chases Every Penny Bank has not been able to answer any of those three questions effectively. Chases Every Penny Bank is another example of a brain trust that creates offensive and ridiculous policies that separate them from desirable customers. Those people fail to understand that every person who walks into a branch is an opportunity for a valuable connection. Distancing oneself or one's enterprise from potential customers by nickel and diming people is self-sabotage. If Chases Every Penny Bank purged itself of people stuck on floor number six and put only level ten people into policy-making positions, it would greatly improve its chances for elevating into thought and market leadership. Currently they seem like a group of petty, greedy, unimaginative people determined to use coercion as their means for opening accounts. Any bank that refuses to conduct business in cash on behalf of its customers has made itself at best less relevant and they are on course to be replaced by someone who understands how to deliver value added service.

The stories in this chapter reflect all-too-common behaviors today. It's foolish for a bank not to accept cash. The excuses related to money laundering are the hallmark of mundane thinkers who create obstacles for clients and potential clients and lack the competency to be competitive with other banks who legally conduct business in cash. Rudeware, coercive behaviors, and greedy policies eventually get exposed. Petty, unimaginative, and incompetent excuses get exposed. Lies get exposed and trust is lost. During an interview with a different large private bank, I asked their self-described elite five person team this question:

> If we place one hundred million dollars under management with you, will you accept full fiduciary responsibility for your advice on what actions to take or not to take?

Their answer was remarkably idiotic and you need to pay attention to their phrasing. Here was the best answer that private bank's top advisors could offer:

> "There is a sufficiency in the world for man's need but not for man's greed. — *Mahatma Gandhi*

"Technically we cannot agree to any fiduciary responsibility. But, we like to think of ourselves as having a fiduciary mindset and we treat all of our customers as if we were fiduciaries."

I then asked them if they were aware that this account would be in California and that the State of California is a mandatory fiduciary standards state. Their response:

"We are aware of that, but our CEO and corporate lawyer disagree with the State of California's position. Therefore, we cannot sign a fiduciary contract with your client."

Yes, it is not only possible, it is actually rather easy to find highly-educated but unwise people in every field of endeavor. Yes, some of them make it all the way up to CEO or head legal counsel, head of marketing, head of new product development, top compliance officer, or top-level government elected positions or agency appointments. We are awash in a sea of impolite, greedy, and unwise people that occupy high-level management, policy-making, and leadership positions. Sometimes it seems to me that the patients really are running the asylum.

With that said, you can separate yourself from every self-limiting, self-centered, rude, greedy or unwise policy or person in your life. If a person or an enterprise insists upon saying or doing that which separates them from connection and engagement with intelligent people including buyers, voters, or clients, let go of them. We live in a time when every second of your life you get to choose whether or not to align yourself with a new and better business or political model, offering, and way of being. If you cannot reform the enterprise you are in, leave it. Join a better enterprise or imagineer your own expression of the next great thing. Become the next great thing. Do it as fast as possible. Please do yourself that favor. Please show yourself, the world and the universe that you refuse to be ordinary and that you are extraordinary. Move yourself to where you want and need to be next before some-one beats you to it.

Chapter Twenty-Two

Transcending Bias, Envy, Resistance, and Unwise Behavior

From late 1979 through 1980 I worked as a salesman in the photocopier and word processor business. I rose rapidly through the ranks, received many bonuses and was targeted by executive recruiters. One of our main competitors offered me a very attractive position that involved an increase in compensation and other benefits that I could not refuse.

I went through a few interviews and was quickly invited to complete the hiring and paperwork process. I decided not to resign from or give notice to my current employer until the final contract had been signed by all parties. That turned out to be a good decision.

While I sat in the Human Resources office filling out the last of the paperwork, the head of the department invited me into her office. She pointed out that I had not completed my college education information. All I had written was that I attended Santa Monica College as a music major for one semester. I confirmed that was all of the college I had attended and that I did not possess a college degree. She looked mortified. She excused herself for a few minutes. She returned with the Senior Vice President that had personally recruited me and insisted that I accept his offer. He was as shocked as I was that their company had a new policy wherein they only hired college graduates. In effect, he had to withdraw the job offer. He was very embarrassed and apologetic.

I asked them if they would re-invite me if I went back to college and finished a four-year degree in music. The head of Human Resources and the Senior Vice President both agreed they would immediately hire me once I had that degree. I asked the Senior Vice President to explain to the head of Human Resources why he wanted me. He told her, "Bruce is awesome at replacing our company's machines. He wins about 80% of the time when we compete with him. We're tired of competing against him. We want him on our team ASAP."

This next part of the conversation was totally unexpected. I asked them if they knew what percentage of our clients and decision makers held four-year college degrees. They both guessed that about 35% of office managers held degrees and probably 60% of business owners held four-year degrees. "Why is that relevant?" asked the Senior Vice President. I answered, "From now on whenever I'm presenting to buyers, I'm going to ask them about college and what they learned there. I'll ask about how valuable their degrees are in the real world. Whenever I deal with people who didn't graduate from college, I'll tell them about my little adventure with your company. I'll ask them how they feel about doing business with a company that would not hire them to sell their machines ... unless they had a four-year college degree ... in music."

I told them that in the past I had not felt any passion for replacing their machines or beating them, but suddenly that had all changed. From then on, I was on a mission to replace their machines. I became their primary nemesis in my territory. I carefully worded that story, refining it into a well-polished arrow in my quiver. I pulled it out with every non-college graduate that made buying decisions. Clients loved my story and they did not appreciate a company that was happy to take their money but too good to employ them. Yes it was emotionally driven. And yes, I used that company's profoundly unwise policy to my advantage. In

> **"The rule for every man is not to depend on the education which other men prepare for him—not even to consent to it, but to strive to see things as they are, and to be himself as he is.** — *Woodrow Wilson*

that market, the machines customers bought or leased were universally equal. The equipment being sold was so similar in performance and price that success depended mostly on personality and emotional connection with the salesperson, follow-up service, and, if possible, the machine. People tend to do business with people they like. People that resonate with them more so than with companies or brands. My success ratio against that competitor climbed to over 90%. I had excellent and competitive machines for customers to enjoy and rely on and people did not care whether or not I had a degree in music.

Over the last few decades, my companies have been paid millions of dollars to train top executives, elite advisors, lawyers, consultants, and salespeople even though I still do not have a college degree in music. Many of those companies wouldn't hire me if I came to them seeking employment because I don't have a degree in something or anything. But, because they seek me out for relevant wisdom and the acquisition of competitive advantages, they are happy to pay us on par with what their top executives earn. Sometimes they will even pay us millions of dollars for licensing agreements that solve their better mousetrap or resonance with clients' challenges.

Like me, you do not need a degree in order to excel or become masterful at something relevant and valuable. For example, I invented Macro Strategic Planning®, Micro Strategic Planning™ and Advanced Macro Wealth Management™

Diamonds are pieces of coal that withstood the adversity and pressure of the world. Their toughness and tenacity enabled them to transform into something stronger, more valuable, and magnificent.

---

and a host of related modalities and intellectual properties. When you are the creator of something, you don't need a degree in that thing or field. When you're the inventor of a whole new market, there are exactly zero educational institutions offering a degree in that. Wise people want results and they are willing to pay for them in cash and sometimes also in equity. Masterful execution of details produces predictable desirable results. Use this story to help you make wiser hiring decisions or to inspire you to create and master something rare or unique that is both relevant and commercially valuable. When you have done that, you will have transcended the relevancy of a college degree.

It's unlikely that anyone who carefully studies this book and talks with our satisfied clients would doubt our credibility on how to achieve thought or market leadership. When it comes to understanding and applying the recipe for transcendence, our track record speaks for itself. Our clients will testify that we are the best in the world at this. Our goal is to always be in the top 0.0001% of people engaged in such professional work.

As this book resonates with millions of people who use it to elevate themselves and those with whom they work to the roof of the building, a university or college is likely to ask me to create a course or use one of my e-courses. After that happens, there will be some who would prefer to hire a person with a degree or certificate in Transcendent Market Leadership rather than me because I still will not have a college degree.

Yes, such a person would most likely possess a college degree in order to be so blinded by the perception of the importance of certificates and degrees. Beauty is found in the eye of the beholder. Sometimes even a doctorate or master's degree does not necessarily make a person wise enough to perceive what ought to be obvious. I'm in favor of advanced and perpetual education, especially in relevant subject matter. That's why I invent constructs and then create education courses for people who want to elevate their knowledge and capacity in those topics. Degrees issued by academia are nice and they can prove to be valuable, but results alter the world and produce fortunes and empires.

As you elevate yourself into thought leadership and market leadership, my life story and journey can provide you with important ideas that translate into your own effectiveness, efficiency, and prosperity. You can learn from my mistakes and successes. That knowledge, well applied, will speed and ease your ascension into greatness.

It is almost inevitable that imposters, resistors, haters, status quo lovers and defenders, and envious people will show up in your life. You can succumb to the pressure and resistance or you can follow my example and choose to remain focused and tenacious in your mission. I have routinely and systematically transcended such resistance, bias, envy, and inanity and so can you. When you become a person well respected for delivering desired tangible results, you will have transcended normalcy and those who seem to worship it.

Chapter Twenty-Three

Stone Soup

I love stories, fables, anecdotes, and metaphors that have proven to be relevant for centuries. One of the ways I exercise and stretch my imagination is by scrutinizing such things. This also helps to increase one's discernment if one is willing to grow it. I love to explore how often they are relevant or true. Then I push myself to see if I can take an old story or fable and build on it to make it more relevant for people living today. Once I learn a story then test and expand it, I am able to see truths about human nature, philosophical, spiritual, business, or financial constructs in new ways. Sometimes ancient wisdom offers the fastest and surest path to understanding current conditions and transcending them.

One of my favorite stories has been interpreted many ways over the past several hundred years. I love how it has been tweaked in so many subtle and not-so-subtle ways. In some cultures it is called "Nail Soup," but its most common title is "Stone Soup."

I believe that every person who wants to be a better leader or steward with themselves and with others needs to be intimately acquainted with this story. The implications related to leadership in every area of life, business, finance, philanthropy, and politics are amazing once you truly understand them. As your awareness and understanding increase, you will see examples of Stone Soup in just about every area of human relations. Someone someplace is attempting to Stone Soup you or someone near you right now and every day that you're alive. Yes, the Stone Soup story is much more than a story. It's a far reaching universal construct that can be used for good or for evil. The big questions about the Stone Soup construct for you are:

- Will you use the Stone Soup construct in ways that are beneficial to others without being coercive or a win for you and a loss for others?

- To what extent will you allow yourself, your business, or net worth to be manipulated by purveyors of the Stone Soup construct?

I have some additional questions for you after you have finished studying my version of the Stone Soup story. Of course, I strongly encourage you to read at least three or more versions of the Stone Soup or Nail Soup story to enrich the depth and breadth of your awareness.

Stone Soup

For thousands of years, soldiers have often found themselves stranded in foreign lands at war's end. Whether they were conquerors or were defeated, many soldiers had to find their own ways back home. This put enormous stress on resources and people all along the path of migration. Farms, ranches, and villages were sometimes overrun and pillaged by home-ward bound soldiers.

Somewhere along the line an ancient tale developed wherein three soldiers, Thomas, Bravus, and Antoine, found themselves without food or money. Each farm or town they came upon claimed to have no food or shelter to offer them. In this desperate state, Antoine the soldier remembered a gift and accompanying lesson presented to him by his uncle.

Antoine's uncle had been a soldier who had suffered the same fate when he was returning from war many years earlier.

As a parting gift, Antoine's uncle had given him a beautiful velvet pouch containing several magical stones. Those stones had been polished smooth over thousands of years lying in a river just waiting for an imaginative and hungry soldier to discover and exploit them for his purposes.

The casual observer might not take any interest in such ordinary looking stones. But Antoine's uncle knew very well their magical qualities and how their magic could affect an entire village.

Antoine decided to show the magical stones to his companions and he taught each of them the roles they were to act out in the next village. They diligently rehearsed their roles as they traveled to the next village. By the time they arrived, it was just about time for dinner. The soldiers were immediately told that the villagers had no food and they should move along down the road to the village beyond.

Antoine told the villagers that they had come prepared with their own food. Then he did something incredible. Antoine invited the entire village to join him and his companions for dinner. The villagers were amazed at this invitation. Never before had any soldiers offered to provide food for the villagers. Soldiers had always taken from them rather than given to them. That is why the villagers hoarded and hid their food so well.

At this point, the mayor asked Antoine what they would be serving. With great enthusiasm Antoine declared, "We shall enjoy my family's most favorite and famous dish. The recipe has been in our family for several generations. It is so revered by the people in my homeland that my great-grandfather was persuaded to open a restaurant so people from all over the world could enjoy it."

Then Bravus chimed in and said, "Yes, it is true. Many times

I have enjoyed Antoine's famous Stone Soup. It is unlike any other soup I have ever tasted."

The mayor's wife inquired where they planned on cooking this grand meal of Stone Soup. Antoine responded rather confidently, "Right here in the village square if we may have your permission to do so. After all we want all of our guests to watch us as we prepare it. That way your entire village will know the recipe and be able to prepare Stone Soup for yourselves for many years to come."

Bravus intervened with this statement, "Antoine, I have never seen you prepare Stone Soup for so many people. Where will you find a cauldron large enough to satisfy the whole village?" Antoine responded, "Bravus, I want everyone to enjoy my Stone Soup. I don't want anyone left out. I wonder if anyone here has a large cauldron they could contribute to help us achieve our goal of feeding the whole village?"

Some of the villagers felt quite concerned that unless a large enough cauldron was contributed, they might not get to enjoy Stone Soup. As the size of the crowd increased, so did the anticipation and the anxiety was building. Then Bob, the owner of the second largest and second most prestigious inn, realized that he must not be left out of this opportunity to promote and possibly elevate his business. He spoke with a loud thunderous voice, "I have two large cauldrons that I want to contribute. I want all of my friends and neighbors to enjoy this world famous Stone Soup." Bob sent his apprentice to fetch the two largest cauldrons and all the bowls and spoons they could gather.

Antoine thanked Bob the innkeeper and asked if he would like to be the first to see the main ingredient. Bob responded, "What is the main ingredient?" Antoine slowly and delicately pulled the velvet pouch from his pocket. Then he took two of the magic stones from their pouch and held them up so Bob and the villagers could see them. Antoine declared, "These are two of the most precious magic stones for making Stone Soup. Soon you will taste soup so wonderful that you will know that only magic stones could produce something so hearty and delicious."

Bravus asked if anyone would like to help him fetch the water needed for the broth. Several volunteers produced buckets and went to the well with Bravus to get the water. Thomas produced several small pouches from his pack and declared, "Antoine, I'm afraid we haven't quite enough herbs and spices for two large cauldrons of Stone Soup. What shall we do?"

The woman who owned the spice shop recognized her opportunity to participate and maybe promote her business just a little. She asked Antoine for a list of spices and herbs, then quickly retrieved them from her shop. By the time she returned, two fires had been built by the villagers and the cauldrons now full of water were warming as they hung above the fires.

Antoine asked for two special volunteers to put one magical stone in each cauldron. Over one hundred villagers raised their hands hoping to be chosen to handle a magical stone and put it in a cauldron. The village butcher saw an opportunity to gain some favor so he inquired, "Antoine, what kind of meat is most suitable for Stone Soup?" Antoine responded by asking the crowd to raise their hands if they wanted meat in their Stone Soup. All raised their hands. Then Antoine asked the butcher what quality of meat he was willing to contribute. Immediately the butcher replied, "Only my very best cuts of elk and venison would be suitable for your world famous Stone Soup."

Not wanting to let such an opportunity to act as a leader pass by, the mayor spoke up and asked if anyone else would be kind enough to contribute some of their gardens' most delicious vegetables. Soon the villagers were offering the very best vegetables from their gardens. There were so many contributions that they would not all fit into the cauldrons, so Thomas and some of the villagers made a fantastic salad with the leftovers. The two competing bakers wanting to promote their businesses each contributed a variety of rolls, breads, and even pastries for dessert.

The soldiers and the villagers enjoyed a hearty meal and an impromptu festival that lasted well into the night. All filled their bellies and shared a wonderful experience. Everyone said that Antoine's soup must be made from magic as they had never before enjoyed such a flavorful and hearty soup.

The innkeeper provided his best rooms for each of the soldiers. Then once the innkeeper had the opportunity to speak with Antoine alone, he offered Antoine ten pieces of silver for the two magic stones. Antoine replied that ten pieces of silver would not be enough to feed and house his companions all the way home. Without his magic stones, they would soon be hungry and financially destitute again. Perceiving this to be a once in a lifetime opportunity, the innkeeper increased his offer to one hundred pieces of silver and Antoine accepted most graciously.

As Antoine and his companions journeyed home, they played out the Stone Soup act several times enchanting villagers, business people and politicians into contributing to the cause of feeding and caring for everyone. Each time they completed a performance, Antoine was approached by an innkeeper or restaurateur who insisted upon buying a magic stone or two or three.

Whenever Antoine ran out of magic stones, he would find a stream bed and search for believable specimens of magic stones. Being a generous man, Antoine paid Bravus and Thomas a fair percentage for the performance of their convincing roles. In this way Antoine, Bravus, and Thomas soon obtained enough wealth to travel in style and return home with a nice amount of cash to begin the next phase of their lives.

In many parts of the world today, you can still find Stone Soup or Nail Soup on menus. Some of the finest inns and restaurants list Stone Soup as their specialty. Many leaders also have some version of Stone Soup on their tactics menu, whether in positive or negative ways.

How have you seen the Stone Soup tactic used in negative manipulative ways in the lives of those you serve as a fiduciary, steward, or leader?

_____

_____

_____

Stone Soup Restaurants

There are many restaurants in the United States named for stone soup, including:

The Stone Kitchen, Atlanta, GA

Stone Soup Café, St. Petersburg, FL

Stone Soup Company, Tampa FL

Stone Soup Market and Café, Landrum, SC

Stone Soup Restaurant, Strafford, VT

Stone Soup Food Company, Kingston, NY

Stone Soup Cafe, Long Beach, CA

Look for one in your area and try its version of stone soup.

"Leadership is the art of getting someone else to do something you want done because he wants to do it. —*Dwight D. Eisenhower*

How could you use the Stone Soup tactic to help others in positive ways, in your role as a person of influence, steward, leader, or fiduciary?

_____

_____

_____

How could you use the Stone Soup tactic to improve circumstances in your personal life and relationships?

_____

_____

_____

How have you seen the Stone Soup tactic used in negative manipulative ways in the lives of those you serve as a fiduciary, steward, or leader?

_____

_____

_____

Because I chose to improve my clarity about positive and negative ways to use the Stone Soup tactic, I became more discerning and able to recognize coercion, manipulation, opaque, or forceful ways for pushing or pulling people into doing things they would not want to do on their own. I also learned to recognize positive, peaceful, transparent, transcendent, and enlightened ways for stewards and leaders to elevate themselves, those connected to them and their respective organizations.

The "incrementalism" in the Stone Soup construct, that is, gaining buy-in one step at a time, can be used for individual or common good, especially when you're using this tactic transparently and the people who are participating are doing so through informed consent. It can be applied in self-serving or deceitful ways to gain power, money or control at the expense of others who are too naïve or programmed to realize they are being abused or disempowered. If one puts on a good enough show and enlists the aid of certain influential people, it becomes rather easy to sell magic stones to under-discerning buyers.

Sometimes incremental progress is the best path to innovation. At times, incremental progress Stone Soup style, combined with hope, faith, and tenacity, is the only way to get from where we are now into a future that could not have been fully or accurately imagined. Oftentimes we must forge ahead without the benefit of a clear path or succinct goals. When the path is unclear, baby steps are often more comfortable and actionable than quantum leaps.

Just as "good enough" is often the enemy of excellence, innovation, and the majestic; incrementalism can as well be the enemy of quantum beneficial change. Deploying the Stone Soup construct can be used to feed a person or a village for a day, but it may slow or restrain people from bold new ideas and actions that will feed them for multiple generations. It has taken me many hours of observation and thought to see this as clearly as I do now.

Knowing when to act incrementally and when to exercise quantum leap innovation or leadership is often a matter of faith combined with discernment. There is no such thing as certainty or safety for innovators or those who wish to remain market leaders. There are times when success depends upon a blend of incremental Stone Soup and a little "magic" combined with jumps and a quantum leap or two. Agility, flexibility, hope, faith, tenacity, and courage along with discernment seem to be essential ingredients. However, the exact amounts and timing are almost always unclear to us humans at the beginning. That is why innovation, thought leadership, and market leadership are grand adventures reserved for those who dare to go where the timid cannot be found.

This is why it is so important that innovators surround themselves with those who are experienced at innovating. People who dare to fail and have failed, but get themselves up again and tenaciously move upward and onward, can speed and ease your journey into thought and market leadership. Surround yourself with these people. Life-long innovators are easy to attract if one is: a) Truly serious about innovating; b) Willing to share some of the glory; and c) Share a reasonably proportionate amount of the treasure.

Chapter Twenty-Four

Stewardship Over Self and With Others

Recently I observed what I call a "Disempowerment Leader" telling the whole world, "Society has abandoned young black people in America." That man probably believes he is helping people, but such an overriding statement only has the power to diminish. It cannot elevate anyone in part because of how false its premise is.

Here is an important dose of perspective intended to help those who believe it and elevate those who apply it:

> Since the beginning of civilization, no society or business has ever abandoned or supported everyone. Even the greatest men and women have detractors. No great leader can please everyone. Some thought leaders were so ardently opposed in their mission that they were tortured, imprisoned, murdered, or martyred. Every individual can choose to connect with society or to disconnect from society according to their own level of consciousness and positive or negative energy and actions. We each decide whether to learn how to live more effectively and abundantly or to live in scarcity, fear, helplessness, and victimhood. That choice is present in our lives each second that we're alive. We can also choose to fool ourselves and those who are easily duped into believing that we can hide in or from the past. We can

blame others for our conditions and feel victimized and bitter. We can decide whether to have an impact on society that's positive and connect in that way or to be a negative influence. American and many other societies are composed of so many diverse ideologies and constructs that it is largely impartial; therefore it's up to us to choose what connection we'll have and what impact we will make for ourselves.

To anyone who feels abandoned by society, or even a company, I offer this invitation:

Every second that you are alive, you choose how connected or disconnected you feel and how you perceive yourself to fit in society. Every second that you are alive, you can learn or create positive ways to have an impact with others or with society. If you do not like the society you are currently connected to, you can move yourself into a different society where you feel more congruent. Or you can impact the society you are in and influence it to move closer into alignment with you. You are a powerful, creative being and you can always imagine and manifest new realities or circumstances without harming or deceiving anyone else.

The next time you hear some disempowerment leader pontificating memes that are disempowering, easily proven to be false, and doom people to failure, remember that you can exercise your own power, imagination, and ability to create what you want next.

Each type of leader attracts a certain type of follower. Every follower is attracted to a certain type of leader. One type of leader is dedicated to helping you discover and align with your highest most capable, powerful, significant, and joyful

Just as my friend, Mark Kastleman, mentioned in Chapter 1, and I found ways to perceive childhood abuse differently and rise above it, so can you.

---

self. That type of leader encourages you to find your own passion, motivation, self-discipline, and courage so you can manifest your highest and best destiny. This type of leader discourages bitterness about the past and excuse making. This type of leader teaches you to stop blaming others or God for present circumstances and encourages you to be the creator of what you want. Elevating and empowering leaders encourage you to look forward rather than backward because what you want next can only be manifested now or in the future. It can't be found or manifested in the past. Hiding in or from the past is a dysfunctional delusion that cannot empower or elevate you or anyone else.

I discussed this book and my views on leadership and stewardship with my friend Ronaldo. What follows is some of what I remember from our conversation. We discussed the spring 2015 rioting in Baltimore Maryland, the conditions that preceded the violence and destruction, and what needed to happen to elevate people out of those circumstances. I commented that far too much emphasis was being put on the past and that disempowerment leaders were doing what they always do — misleading people further into bitterness, despair, and victimhood while they gained fame, power, influence, and money for themselves.

Ronaldo: "Bruce, you have to consider the past. You can't lose sight of things like oppression, slavery, bigotry, and circumstances that limit people."

Bruce: "Ronaldo, you say you can't lose sight of them and I'm saying you must lose sight of them if you are to elevate

"I don't think of myself as a poor deprived ghetto girl who made good. I think of myself as somebody who, from an early age, knew I was responsible for myself, and I had to make good. —*Oprah Winfrey*

beyond them. A runner constantly looking over his shoulder is likely to stumble and fall. Looking backward slows you down. It puts you at risk and diminishes your chances of winning your race or achieving your personal best time at a given distance. A sailor unwilling to lose sight of the California coast will not arrive in Hawaii."

Ronaldo went on to suggest that our past makes us who we are today and those who are born into poverty or with darker skin or whose ancestors were slaves are at an extreme disadvantage. Ronaldo has a huge compassionate heart and wants everyone to live a peaceful, abundant, and joyful life just as much as I do. Our conversation continued:

Bruce: "Were any of your ancestors enslaved?"

Ronaldo: "Yes. I'm Jewish and over the centuries my ancestors were enslaved and even slaughtered by the millions. They were abused by bigots, disrespected, and were denied access to opportunities that were readily available to others. Some of that bigotry, disrespect, and denial of opportunity still goes on today."

Bruce: "Some of my ancestors were enslaved by the Romans. Many of my Irish ancestors were abused and oppressed by the English. My Scottish ancestors were abused and oppressed by the English. Some of my English ancestors could very well have been oppressive tyrants and slave owners. White on white slavery, bigotry, oppression, and denial of opportunity is every bit as hurtful and wrong as when people of different skin colors do so to each other.

When my Irish ancestors immigrated to America, they were victimized in many ways by greedy men, tyrants, oppressors, and bigots. Despite all of that mistreatment and horrible impoverished circumstances, some of them found ways to rise above all of that. Some learned a new mindset, awareness, and behavioral model that empowered them to elevate out of ignorance and the vicious claws of failure, victimhood, hopelessness, despair, and poverty."

Ronaldo: "Wow, I rarely if ever look back at my family history and how we were oppressed and victimized. I don't allow the modern bigots and oppressors to impact who I am or impede my progress.

Bruce: "Being aware of the past is important because of what we can learn from it, but if we're taught and believe a perpetual victimization or failure story about the past that limits us now and in the future, we allow ourselves to be held captive by the past.

People make up stories constantly. We're taught certain stories, perspectives and beliefs by parents, teachers, coaches, our friends and their parents, etcetera. But each of us gets to choose what stories, perspectives, and beliefs we will live with now and next. Remember that all stories are filtered by flawed and fragile human beings. They tell us those stories from their own limited and incomplete perspective. They don't perceive anything with perfect understanding and neither do we.

Great leaders and wise, effective stewards help us create or adopt stories, perspectives, and beliefs that empower us now and help us elevate ourselves. Awareness of history is most beneficial when we use it to empower ourselves and others now and into the future. We can adopt an empowering and elevating story or narrative about the past rather than one that limits us and those around us. You and I are not our ancestors and we don't have to be held hostage by their limiting or ineffective beliefs or mistakes. We have chosen not to be limited by oppressive tyrants or enslavers past or present. That is essential to transcending limiting beliefs and circumstances.

So, I suggest this: When we do look back, we need to find positives despite all of the negatives and use them as positive energy now and moving forward, upward and onward. We can write our own stories and perspectives on the past. When we do that, we can draw power from the past that we can use as fuel now and into the future.

Effective self-stewardship demands that we let go of all of the stories, people, memes, and constructs that diminish us as individuals, families, or societies. This can be accomplished in ways that are loving, polite, and gentle with our psyches and souls. Wherever you are today is largely the byproduct of what you believed and what you did or didn't do in the past and of the positive or negative beliefs and actions of others. Where you are now is also the outgrowth of occurrences, circumstances, and people outside of your influence or control. What matters most right now is what type of energy, beliefs, behaviors, and impact you are choosing and applying now and next. Those who feel destined to live in failure, ignorance, scarcity, poverty, and weakness have not yet learned what empowering thoughts to think, how to think with discernment, proportion, and balance, and how to act powerfully and abundantly. It is important that you detach yourself from the beliefs and behaviors that ensnare those stuck in the basement of the ten-floor building if you want to experience life on its sixth floor. If you want to experience life on the roof of the penthouse, you must learn and emulate the thinking and behaviors that empower transcendent elevation — most of which are well outside the awareness of those people muddling through life on the sixth floor.

Stewardship With Others

A sense of stewardship with others elevates leaders into the highest level of effectiveness. Elevated leadership occurs when the steward isn't lording over those for whom the steward is responsible. I have acted as a steward in many ways with lots of people. Over the decades my ongoing desire to improve my effectiveness at achieving desired outcomes led me to let go of the idea that I was a steward over others. As I evolved into a construct where all of us were in it together striving for clarity, alignment, and agreed upon goals, each project flowed better. Manifesting positive desired results became more common and disappointments occurred less frequently. As I helped those around me to understand how their highest and best interest was at stake, people, even children, were more cooperative and they contributed more positive energy because they understood and felt a stronger whole brain, whole being connection with the outcome. They felt and became more engaged with a co-created and co-actualized plan than they would feel with a plan dictated by me. Even the most benevolent dictators usually end up being resented and are often stripped of their power. Most, but not all, humans prefer independence and self-realization over tyranny or being dismissed as too unwise to understand, protect, and further their own best interests.

By setting an example of how clarity, focus, self-discipline, courage, and tenacity could be exercised or expressed in the accomplishment of goals, many participants did the same. Even people who didn't consider themselves to be strong, capable, disciplined, courageous, and tenacious, or worthy of success began experiencing more success. That led to more people feeling competent and confident enough to be worthy of success. I believe that shifting away from lording over them to working with them changed hearts and minds in positive ways. It produced a more positive flow of energy.

It helped people increase their own power. It helped expand their own imaginations so they became better at overcoming challenges without our oversight and powerful enough to manifest their own as well as shared goals.

When a steward helps guide people into higher levels of awareness and engagement, it's only natural that the participants begin to exercise more of their own power and personal majesty. The manifestation of real tangible results brings people together unlike any theory or practice. Solutions that are self-discovered and positive outcomes self-manifested are at least sticky. They can even become extremely enduring, as is the case with principles-based 500-1,000 year plans. If you view and act upon your stewardship in this way, you will help elevate the people around you. If that isn't payoff enough, doing so will increase your cash flow, reduce complaints, and increase equity value. This is an example of every contributor winning in ways that personally matter.

Martin Luther King, Jr. exercised his stewardship in that way. Gandhi accomplished his mission peacefully through this type of stewardship. Jesus Christ, arguably the most masterful steward in history, used the sort of gentle loving compassionate construct I have articulated in this chapter. I find it informative that the Lord of heaven and earth did not use his power to lord over people. Instead Jesus invited people to ignite passion and purpose within their own souls. The followers of Christ have been attempting, with varying degrees of success, to apply his teachings and invitation to elevate themselves upward and onward for thousands of years. Whether you are a Christian or not (Jesus was a Jew and Gandhi was Hindu), you can apply elevating and inviting methods of stewardship and leadership to improve circumstances and outcomes for yourself and others.

Chapter Twenty-Five
Proportionality

Comprehending proportion in any type of human relationship is important. All too often proportionality is misunderstood. Sometimes it is intentionally misrepresented by people in order to further a flawed ideology, false narrative, or to increase a personal win at the expense of others. To actually live a win-win existence, rather than merely claiming to do so, one must become adept at understanding proportional contributions, benefits, and wins for each participant in a relationship.

Fairly early in my career as an innovator and influencer I did not know how to recognize, appreciate, and monetize my contributions to business relationships. In many instances my enterprises or I received far too little compensation in cash or equity. Because of my youthful inexperience and the absence of support and protection that could have been provided by A-level advisors in my life, I routinely allowed buyers and customers or clients to establish price and terms and to under value the impact of my contributions. I allowed them to arbitrarily pull numbers out of thin air and I let them determine what my wins would be. Sometimes I fell for the old "We can't pay you for your contributions of time, energy, and intellectual property, or wisdom but the exposure to our audience will be good for you. That exposure will bring you cash flow and other benefits." Such a construct is usually offered by people who are greedily focused on their own wins at the expense or to the detriment of other contributors. Sometimes it's merely an indication of an intellectual or emotional laziness that prevents people from understanding and applying win-win solutions. Once I came to understand how precious my time, talents, contributions, influence, and impact were to the prosperity of other parties, I became more effective at establishing proportionate win-win relationships. I also stopped representing myself in negotiations and retained extremely competent representation dedicated to protecting and furthering my firm's best interests.

Here is an important truth about win-win that will help you optimize your own success in business, while making sure that all participants win:

> Each participant is responsible for understanding the proportionality of their own contributions and the appropriate amount of benefits derived from them. Then each participant is responsible for articulating and justifying their proportional contributions as well as the benefits they expect the others involved to derive. This must be articulated in detail in writing, including timing, various benchmarks, cash flow, equity when appropriate, and non-financial considerations. Each participant needs to understand what is going in and what is coming out.

Not being able to understand that fundamental truth meant that I didn't apply it. So I was undercompensated relative to the value I created or manifested for others. But that wasn't the worst price of my ignorance. Here is the worst part:

As I awakened to my proportionate value and began speaking up for compensation I deserved, some of my strategic allies, clients, and customers tried to devalue what were irrefutable tangible results including the cash flow I created for them.

Some of them had increased their cash flow by tens of millions of dollars in only a year or two; yet I had allowed them to devalue my contributions moving forward. When I began to change my business model into something more long term and proportionally appropriate, they insisted that they should not have to continue paying training or licensing fees. Paying my firm an ongoing licensing fee seemed ridiculous to some of them because they were choosing not to grasp the value and proportionality of my past, ongoing, or future contributions. Some people are intentionally blind to the value contributed by others while they can clearly see the value of their own contributions. Such people tend to love and adore you right up until they have to pay you proportionately. Some people anxiously look for a way to end your involvement and compensation as soon as possible and they will devalue past contributions — even those past contributions that substantially led to their success or that continue to prosper them.

As my awareness increased, some of my supporters, clients, and allies appreciated my ability to recognize and articulate my proportionate value. They even admired my new methods for empowering myself to be compensated in proportion to the wins I created or manifested for them. My reach, influence, and proven ability to manifest very real tangible results that truly mattered to them meant that we could all agree on an increase in speaking, training, or licensing fees. Those who chose not to recognize the value of the results wanted to hide behind claims such as:

1. "Bruce, my friend, nobody in their right mind is going to pay you $100,000 for a keynote speech, let alone three million dollars for thirty speeches and training sessions per year."

2. "I agree that your intellectual properties, influence, and mentoring made us millions that we would not have

> **The reality today is that we are all interdependent and have to co-exist on this small planet. Therefore, the only sensible and intelligent way of resolving differences and clashes of interests, whether between individuals or nations, is through dialogue.** — *The Dalai Lama*

made last year without you, but I only have $200,000 in my entire training budget and I can't pay you more than a quarter of those funds."

3. "The SEC, FINRA, or our Board of Directors, or my spouse won't let us pay you what you want or think that you are worth."

As lovingly and gently as possible I simply withdrew my influence and connection from those who could not or would not pay a fair and proportional share of initial and ongoing revenue and benefits. Today I choose to work with people who possess creative imaginations and enough business acumen and financial awareness to understand proportional contributions and how to effectively monetize them for everyone involved. Sometimes this involves a combination of cash and equity up front, then additional cash and equity as benchmarks are achieved or passed. Talented merger and acquisition professionals and executive compensation specialists can always come up with deals that respect proportional contributions, influence, and impact. Brilliant leaders will not allow themselves or their enterprises to be stuck in the status quo and mediocrity over money. The brightest people and the greatest leaders know how and where to get the capital and/or financing necessary to acquire what they need to become market leaders. At the very least they know who to call to help them obtain it.

Increased proportional awareness is necessary for anyone who wants to understand value and monetize it in win-win ways. Innovation, influence, reach, and elevation will have a financial and possibly some kind of emotional price. Especially when negotiating acquisition agreements or the sale of assets or intellectual properties. Remaining in the status quo has both a price and a cost that wise and great leaders refuse to pay. The first buyout offer for my enterprise came from a client. It was unsolicited and unexpected. We turned down that $6 million all cash offer. A year later another client offered us an unsolicited cash offer for $14 million, which we turned down. In both cases our relationships with those who made the offers became stronger and more profitable via enhanced training, speaking or licensing contracts. We figured out how to more accurately define our influence and impact defining them as proportionate wins. This helped each of us succeed at more significant levels.

Our most recent unsolicited offer came from a huge company headquartered in Europe. Opening bid was $42 million in cash. Our next unsolicited offer will likely be for much more than that. I cannot say for certain what the terms of the offer will be, but I do know that we are too experienced to allow our intellectual property or company to be purchased solely out of our own future cash flow. Any acceptable deal will be proportionally accurate and fair for everyone involved. Capable experienced business people dedicated to achieving and sustaining market dominance will be able to optimize global distribution and revenue from our transcendent intellectual properties. If you want to badly enough, you will create or acquire intellectual properties, products, or services that you can monetize and use to move into market leadership. If I could do this, so can you.

> **"When you show deep empathy toward others, their defensive energy goes down, and positive energy replaces it. That's when you can get more creative in solving problems.** —*Stephen R. Covey*

Between now and the time we sell or merge my enterprise and IP, we will continue to offer proportionally correct licensing agreements, training programs, speeches, influence, and impact. Those who can comprehend the value of impact on their bottom lines due to our outside and innovative influence will understand, agree with, and pay my enterprise accordingly. You can also do this with your IP if you come to understand proportionate value, how to describe it, and how to effectively monetize it in ways that are win-win. It would also be wise to learn from my earlier mistakes. Don't repeat my mistakes. Surround yourself with client-centered masterful advisors and allow them to negotiate the best price and terms for you. Get out of your own way. Stop being the biggest limiting factor in your life, business, or financial well-being.

I currently offer a combination of one–to-many and one-on-one training and mentoring for groups of business leaders who want to improve effectiveness at monetizing their products, intellectual properties, influence, and wisdom. Of course, all of our price points are fair, win-win, and proportional. Because each project is at least somewhat unique, individual clients who want customized help receive contracts that reflect specific proportionally fair pricing and terms.

A different type of example of how to apply proportionality as a competitive advantage is the Vaughan Benz company. Like many of my friends, Scott Vaughan and David Benz, the owners of Vaughan Benz, came into my life as clients. They have built one of America's most successful premium furniture manufacturers. They serve two primary market segments: 1) Four star and higher hotels; and 2) Very discerning individuals who desire exquisite custom furniture.

In order to satisfy the massive orders from elite hotels, David and Scott outsource *some* of the manufacturing to artisans outside of America. David and Scott were early pioneers in partnering with Chinese and Vietnamese companies, artisans, and designers. Two of their great advantages are: 1) Extremely high integrity; and 2) Proportionality. Since this chapter is about proportionality, I'll reveal, with their permission, how they made this a competitive advantage.

Many Americans are stuck in the "our country and culture is superior to everyone else's" frame of mind. Those stuck in that attitude quickly reveal that sentiment to potential partners, allies, clients, and vendors. David and Scott have separated their enterprise and themselves from arrogant players in this way:

They fully invest themselves in gaining an understanding of and in valuing the culture and business constructs of those with whom they interact. They put forth a proportion of themselves into foreign relations that almost none of their competitors seem to be willing to match. This readily comes across to the people in foreign lands with whom they do business. David and Scott demonstrate long-term interest in mutual success. Because of this they don't look, feel, or act like exploitive people. Scott and David contribute a disproportionately high amount of themselves into the creation of multi-cultural respectful business and personal relationships. Add to this an unusually high level of personal and professional integrity and the result is long-term trusting relationships that transcend many of the barriers that cause others to give up on cross-border cross-cultural relationships.

Demonstrating that you understand and care about customers, allies, partners, and vendors proportionately above what your competitors are able or willing to do can be a profound competitive advantage. Remember this:

People do business with other people more so than with companies, brands, or advertising claims.

When you disproportionately give yourself to mastery of your trade, relationships, understanding, and integrity; discerning people take notice. People will routinely choose to do business with you over competitors as long as your mousetrap and pricing are competitive. This is especially important for you when your offerings are very similar or the same as what competitors offer.

Disproportionate contributions of self, understanding, empathy, integrity, and commitment to win-win can be your competitive advantages. These are available to everyone committed to market leadership. But very few people actually live this way. You can be different in this way and it can make a lot of difference in your ability to ascend into market prominence.

Chapter Twenty-Six

Transcending Addictions and Habits that Limit You and Others

Habitual thoughts and behaviors that are good for you elevate you, stretch your imagination, empower you to create new solutions, and manifest positive outcomes. They might even be good for society if you are bold enough to share them with the world, with or without personal profit. Fortunately you and others reading and studying this book's content have already exposed your psyche to ideas that, when acted upon intelligently and passionately, have the power to elevate you beyond competitors. While many of your competitors have been studying and memorizing fantasy sports related statistics or shopping for new shoes and handbags, you have been nourishing your intellect and soulfully stretching yourself in ways that average minds cannot even imagine.

Throughout my adult lifetime and within the pages of this book, I've been inviting and encouraging everyone to sever the restraints that bind them to ineffectiveness. I've been raising awareness about how affection of or acceptance of mediocrity and the status quo impede innovation and greatness. Some of my friends are experts at overcoming limiting or destructive habits and addictions. One example is my friend Mark B. Kastleman.

Mark is a Clinical Chaplain with a specialty in behavior-change and addiction recovery. As a Spiritual & Mental Health Counselor, Trainer and Mentor, Mark specializes in helping individuals, couples, families and organizations overcome difficult-to-change habits and behaviors, including addiction. Mark is a big believer in the natural-built-in ability of every human being to change for the better and rise from the ashes of extreme challenge, trauma, and addiction. As you read in chapter one, Mark was a victim of child abuse and he transcended that trauma.

Mark is an avid creator and presenter of unique and exciting education and training programs that help people understand their emotions, thought processes, behaviors, habits, and addictions. Mark has a special passion for Neuroscience, the Science of the Heart, and the Art of Spirituality. Most importantly, Mark is all about the simple, practical how-to of directing the heart and mind to recover and continually improve one's life, relationships, and world.

My friend, Dr. David Gruder, is collaborating with me to help people transcend the programming and addiction to ideologies and traditions that separate them from prosperity, sense of significance, and real joy. My intellectual properties related to 100-1,000 year business, family, and macro wealth optimization planning are saturated with elevating constructs that transcend the beliefs and ignorance that tie people to scarcity, fear, dysfunction, and misery. Yes even multi-millionaires, and especially their children and grandchildren, have little or no idea how to construct well-articulated, legally-sound plans that teach and reinforce optimal effectiveness for multiple generations. Yes even very wealthy people can be subsisting in a state of ill-at-ease mind, insignificance, dysfunction, or misery.

Consider this:

To bring into reality your highest best self and
the most significant fulfilling life that you dare to
imagine, you must fully comprehend the differences

between wants and needs. Most heroin addicts are sure what they need is a lifetime of unlimited free heroin. Those of us with un-addled brains know that more heroin is exactly what they do not need if they are to move into alignment with highest best self.

The absence of addiction to every harmful substance, belief, tradition, person, and behavior is essential for those who sincerely desire to experience life in a majestic way of being. Naturally this relates to self-growth and stewardship over self. The absence of addictions improves your attractiveness as a leader. Being free from destructive addictions inspires those you lead to set themselves free and become more effective, productive, and majestic.

One of our success stories is the stewardship of Allen Thomas. When we first met Allen he was immersed in several limiting beliefs and behaviors. I won't go into them in any detail out of respect for his privacy. What I can tell you is this: Allen was having trouble with a company that was victimizing him and disrespecting him. Allen also felt underappreciated by some of his clients and colleagues.

For Allen, and anyone else including you and me, to succeed, it is necessary to outgrow or transcend any connection to victimhood, entitlement, and self-pity. Part of what I love about Allen is how boldly and quickly he courageously elevates his beliefs and his actions. Allen follows directions extremely well, especially when he is given a recipe for success. I could brag on about the excellent self-steward that Allen has grown himself into, but I won't. Instead I secured Allen's permission to include an article about Self Stewardship that briefly describes his own journey.

Stewardship Over Self
By Allen August Thomas

There is little doubt that we live in a turbulent uncertain time in American history. However, as I reflect on history, I cannot think of a time that was not turbulent. In regards to certainty, it seems that most if not every respected philosopher throughout history warned us that certainty (much like absolute safety) is a grand illusion. My new age friends like to think that humanity is on the verge of some really significant breakthroughs that will bring an end to war, bigotry, envy, hatred, and crime. I am told it is some kind of vibrational occurrence in the universe, but I'm not buying it.

It seems to me that humanity is operating at about the same level of dysfunction as it was in the days of Socrates. Many people are still ruled by emotion and easily proven to be false beliefs about themselves, the people around them, and the societies in which they live. Lots of people are immersed in hopelessness, poverty, physical illness, and ill at ease mind, just as it has been since the beginning of time. Then there are some of us operating a level or two above that. We make an honest living, pay our bills, and invest for a "rainy day" and our eventual retirement.

A couple of years ago I decided to really investigate "The American Dream." I wanted to see if it was still possible for someone such as me to significantly improve my financial condition and well-being. As I searched for guidance, I found a litany of self-proclaimed "experts" and "gurus" promising immediate and easy success. They provided "free" webinars that always led to an internet mini course for $197 and a better course for $1,997 and the super premium course for $9,997. Of course they all accepted every major credit card. They all offered some quick fix with "cheat sheets," proven formulas and secret tactics that only really successful people know.

Then one day I met a very unusual man named Bruce

> **I have absolutely no pleasure in the stimulants in which I sometimes so madly indulge. It has not been in the pursuit of pleasure that I have periled life and reputation and reason. It has been the desperate attempt to escape from torturing memories, from a sense of insupportable loneliness and a dread of some strange impending doom.** —*Edgar Allan Poe*

Raymond Wright who told me this:

> Allen, if you want real success, the kind that transcends money and empowers you to live a significant joyful life, you won't find it on some "cheat sheet" for $197. Real success, the kind that endures for multiple generations, hundreds or even thousands of years, will require you to unlearn a lot of what you believe is true. You will have to replace every one of your faulty dysfunctional beliefs about yourself, your ancestors, your community, and your profession. You will need to replace every limiting or restraining belief with new beliefs that elevate your thinking and behavior beyond anything you can understand in your present state of mind.

Although Bruce's words made sense to me, I decided to be offended and I chose a series of courses and gurus that told me how amazing I already was. They promised easy and fast success with almost no work on my end. Every minute and penny invested in their flattery and false promises actually moved me further away from my real goals.

Eventually I called Bruce and we delved deeply into why

I was chasing clients and opportunities when I would rather be attracting them. We explored my stewardship over myself, with my family and with my clients. I quickly discovered that I really did not understand my role as a steward with my wife and children or with my clients. I could not even articulate how I was succeeding or failing as a steward over my own emotional, spiritual, physical, and intellectual well-being.

Every mentoring session with Bruce led me to discover certain limiting beliefs that separated me from the success I wanted. Bruce helped me Self Discover new ideas, beliefs, and constructs that I earnestly applied. As I increased my stewardship ability over my emotions and limiting beliefs, I moved myself into a way of being that is attractive to the kinds of clients and types of projects I had long wanted but could not connect with.

One of my biggest breakthroughs came when I finally admitted to myself and verbally to Bruce that a sense of victimhood was holding me back. It was suppressing the greatness that existed within me. Feeling like a bitter victim was not getting me from where I was to where I wanted to be. Victimhood and bitterness was not attracting into my life the people and opportunities I believed I was suitable for. As I let go of the beliefs and behaviors that produced my old circumstances and embraced more enlightened choices, I produced better outcomes.

Bruce taught me a series of constructs and action steps that moved me into alignment with what I wanted. As I became what my definition of "ideal clients" needed someone to be... they began to find me. I became attractive to them. I no longer had to chase what I wanted or needed. As I applied the new constructs and behaviors, I gained clients in other states. My business went from local to regional to national. Most importantly, I applied the new beliefs and behaviors with my family. As my stewardship with family elevated, those relationships flourished.

In preparation for this article, I asked Bruce if he would contribute a few paragraphs about stewardship over self and transcending limiting beliefs. This is what he provided:

> Whether you realize this or not, anyone tying you to the idea that you are some kind of victim is in fact separating you from your highest, freest, and most powerful self. Anyone (including you) who is looking backward towards how, why, or when you (or your ancestors) have been victimized is distracting you from your deepest, most passionate and imaginative soulful connection with who, what, or where you want to be now and *next*.

> Considering yourself to be a victim (and feeling bitter about it) engulfs you in negative energy and it restrains or blocks you from your clarity of purpose and the positive energy necessary to fuel you towards your highest most powerful self. You get to choose which kind of energy flows through you. You get to choose your friends, heroes and mentors. You get to choose your emotional state of being and you get to choose what if anything you will do about your current and future direction. You will *never* be able to change what actually happened in the past, but you do get to choose what stories you create or believe about the past. You are the one who chooses what kind of energy to take (positive or negative) from the past. You will be the sole decider regarding what type of energy you will apply now and next.

> *You* can politely disengage *yourself* from loved ones, teachers, heroes, "community leaders," politicians and mentors that are (knowingly or unwittingly)

tying you to victimhood and disempowerment. This is about you choosing the stories or writing the stories that tie you down or that elevate you. This is about *you* choosing to out think destructive or disempowering emotions, beliefs and people or being held hostage by them. The key to unlocking your restraints can only be found in *your* own heart, mind, and soul. Only you can free yourself and lead yourself into your highest most powerful self. *You* are the most powerful steward and leader in *your* life, relationships, business and financial endeavors. You must stop giving up your power and abdicating responsibility for the life you say you want now and next. You must become your own best advocate and BE the author and steward of the best future you dare to imagine.

In my next article I will focus on Stewardship With Others vs. Stewardship Over Others. I can hardly wait for you to get that information so you can improve your results with those for whom you have responsibility. Your questions and ideas about this article are important to me. Helping people elevate into greater abundance and wellbeing is my passion. With that end in mind, I invite you to attend one of my speeches or training session or to listen to one of my radio interviews.

* * *

Allen August Thomas uses his passion for helping people optimize self-stewardship and stewardship with others every day. Allen helps his audiences and clients gain clarity about their most important goals. He guides their development of written plans to achieve their greatest desires in life and with family, career, wealth creation, management and preservation. Allen also helps people become better connected to healthy passions, charitable endeavors, stewardship, and leadership.

Allen's clients rave about his rare ability to help them discover imaginative ideas and solutions as he helps them transcend difficulties and manifest more abundant joyful lives. Allen has aligned himself and his business with some of the world's most respected thought leaders and providers of solutions who help people maximize their results.

* * *

Allen has replaced many limiting beliefs and behaviors with far more productive constructs and actions. Similar to my own journey, Allen realizes that as he gets closer to mastery, new questions and awakenings are revealed. As perpetual students, Allen and I concentrate our efforts on learning and improving every day.

Sufficient Willingness, Toughness, and Tenacity

Several years ago, I hired a well-educated and accomplished man who we'll call Ralf. During his initial interview, Ralf told me of his addiction to sex. He promised me that he was following all of the protocols for transcending that addiction and that he would prove to be the smartest hire of my life. I decided to take a chance on Ralf. It proved to be a huge mistake. The straw that broke the camel's back was beyond my imagination. Here is what happened. A client Ralf had been assigned to help called me in a panic to let me know that this highly educated man, Ralf, had done something incredibly offensive the prior afternoon. In between meetings at the client's office, Ralf had been given a traveling executive's office to use for an hour so he could work in private. Instead of working, Ralf spent his time using that executive's computer to log into his account with a company that matches wealthy men with needy women who will become their girlfriends or mistresses for a monthly stipend.

When the executive returned and logged into his computer, he saw a lot of nude pictures and emails with very explicit conversations between Ralf and some of the women he was interviewing. It gets worse. That executive is a very staunch Christian and opponent of prostitution and pornography in any form. He was outraged that his computer was now connected in any way to that website or any of the people involved. He demanded that Ralf be fired immediately. Now his boss, our client, was in a panic because: a) He was also deeply offended at Ralf's behavior; b) That executive was very important to the enterprise; and c) Ralf had proven himself to be essential to the completion of the $20 million merger that was in process. Quite a pickle indeed.

I called Ralf and asked him to meet me in our conference room that afternoon. During that afternoon's interview Ralf opened up, at least partially, and told me that the thousands of dollars in fraudulent charges on his corporate credit card were actually related to gifts, hotels, and meals for his lady friends. Ralf had stopped all efforts to transcend his addiction. He said, "Bruce, the worst thing about it is the lying or maybe it's the stealing. I lie to my wife outright a few times a day. Then there are the lies of omission. I exhausted all of my own wealth a few years ago. My wife inherited a huge fortune and doesn't pay close attention to it. I've burned through hundreds of thousands of dollars of her inheritance to support my mistresses. The lying and stealing is so stressful that it's actually causing me physical dysfunction. So I have to take blue pills in order to perform. The stress-related medications are causing further complications. In short, my addiction is actually killing me but I can't stop and I don't want to stop." Ralf cost my firm millions of dollars in lost opportunity. A little later on Ralf confessed that he and one of his mistresses had conspired in the theft of my credit and identity.

What hurt the most was my psyche. I had overinvested my

faith in him. I spent inordinate amounts of time mentoring him and I was loyal to him right up until the bitter end. He begged me not to prosecute him for the identity and financial theft. Ralf said that he would repay what he and one of his mistresses had stolen. Instead he disappeared and moved out of California and out of my life. The last I heard about him, the IRS had charged him with multiple crimes. He was convicted and sent to prison for tax evasion.

I learned many things from my experiences with that man but I have not lost my ability to be optimistic with and about people. I still give people opportunities to succeed. However, now I rely upon trained professionals paid by my company to evaluate and manage the progress of those with strong obsessions or addictions. Part of what I have learned about people with addictions is this: they can be so overcome by their addiction(s) that they lose the ability to be honest with themselves, their loved ones, employers, colleagues, and clients.

Rather than allowing myself, or my enterprise, to get sucked into the problems that addicts create, we diligently follow every federal and state legal protocol. We entrust the monitoring of their personal progress, and if necessary termination of their employment, to wise and compassionate professionals. Their priority is the protection of my enterprise, our clients, and employees while still dealing with addicts in kindly and legally sound ways. Sooner or later, leaders come face-to-face with mental illness, addiction, and a plethora of dysfunctional attitudes and behaviors. The larger an enterprise grows and the more global it becomes, the more troubled people will be employed. Laws vary from state to state and country to country. For a leader to optimize effectiveness at the highest levels and down throughout the entire enterprise, delegation to masterful experts is essential. Furthermore, it is essential that every leader does whatever is needed to transcend their own obsessions, addictions, limiting attitudes and behaviors. Leading by example is far more powerful than preaching high standards and falling well below them. Or as Ralph Waldo Emerson put it so well, "Who you are speaks so loudly I can't hear what you're saying."

I leave you with this observation:

Families, businesses, and even entire cultures are connected to individual character. They are reflections of the worst behaviors tolerated and the highest behaviors lived by and rewarded by the leaders. Every leader is a steward of the morality of their culture. Leaders set the examples whether they diminish or elevate the consciousness, morality, and effectiveness of their cultures.

Chapter Twenty-Seven

Transcendent Philanthropy

Like many people close to my age, my first experience donating money to and raising money for charity were actualized through the March of Dimes. As far back as I can remember I have believed that helping the helpless is good for everyone involved. Giving to causes that comfort, support, or help to heal people, animals, and the planet bring me into connection with a certain soulful element of significance and joy, especially when it is all done anonymously.

It seems as though there are millions of charities asking us for contributions of time, talent, and of course money. Over the past four decades I have been involved with quite a few charities as a donor, a steward, an ally, or connector, or some combination of those roles.

In the early 1980s I invested myself in learning everything possible related to philanthropy. I diligently studied business and individual tax implications, strategies, tactics, and tools. Every aspect of financial details as well as big picture strategic thinking and planning for individuals, families, businesses, and both public and private foundations fascinated me. By the time I was thirty years old I had taught many continuing education courses all over the U.S.A. to lawyers, CPAs, CFPs, business agents, trust officers, and just about every type of financial advisor and insurance agent. I even taught a four-hour continuing education course for real estate agents throughout California and a few other states.

I became a thought leader and market leader in the area of philanthropy because I had a very rare perspective and I could condense extremely complicated details into understandable, resonant, and actionable benefits for donors. When I first entered that arena in 1985, professional fundraisers who were compensated by charities or lawyers who were paid by charities provided most of the training for professionals. What my due diligence revealed was this:

> All of the courses were full of bias and selective disclosure that maximized as many benefits as possible for the charities in ways that too often diminished benefits to the donors.

What a shock right? Imagine that, human beings were doing what human beings tend to do. Those who ran charities or received compensation to raise money for them created programs that marketed charitable trusts and a variety of deferred and immediate donation tactics that often omitted important details and facts essential to optimizing benefits for the donors. Promoters often chose not to inform students or donors about options such as private family foundations, community foundation partnerships, and donor advised funds. When donors or their more astute advisors brought those options up for discussion with fundraisers, they were often dismissed as being too costly or complicated. This happened even though those options are not any more complicated or costly to manage than other constructs within the existing comfort zone of most affluent discerning people.

To help advisors and donors transcend the schemes and dismissals of such promoters, we developed and taught client/donor-centered courses. I taught my audiences and students what I am teaching you now:

Whenever anyone claims that an option should be dismissed because it is just too complicated for your little brain to understand or it is too expensive for you, politely insist upon seeing a detailed side-by-side comparative analysis that describes advantages, benefits, and possible disadvantages. Demand to see an analysis that demonstrates how the math works specifically for you, with and without whatever is being proposed.

Consumers and client-centric advisors loved our courses and the transparency we brought to the world of philanthropy. Our students and clients flooded our firm with unsolicited referrals in part because of our extreme technical competency and especially because we are demonstrably client-centered and non-conflicted. Many advisors referred clients to us in part because we understood how to help them and their businesses become more helpful and profitable by educating their clients about client-centered philanthropy. The only detractors we had were professional fundraisers and certain employees of charities who viewed us as a threat to their programs. We were disruptive to the defenders and promoters of the charity-centric status quo who did not appreciate our win-win balanced modalities.

To be optimally effective in charitable giving, advisors and their discerning clients need to be supported by professionals who are thoroughly familiar with all of the options available. They need to be masterful at the financial and legal issues and how they impact the client's big picture over multiple generations, as in our 100-1,000 year plans. Supporting professionals also need to be masterful at understanding and empowering their clients emotionally and even spiritually. Assembling a truly client-centered, highly-qualified team that truly understands the client helps assure the protection of the clients' best interests in balance with the charitable intent and the ongoing success of charities with whom the clients have partnered.

The day after my mother passed away on 10/31/2013, I decided to keep a lunch meeting an advisor had arranged for me. Leszek Burzynski ("Lesh"), a cancer-survivor and a highly accomplished film director and producer, was in the process of creating a charity whose purpose is to help people make important decisions that would prepare them to experience a peaceful death. Lesh and I formed a profound connection almost immediately. There I was dealing with the very unexpected death of my mother and sitting across the table from me was a man dedicated to helping everyone transcend death-related grief and anxiety.

Soon after meeting Lesh, I was introduced to Terry Sweeney, Lesh's Co-Founder of IMmortal Foundation. It is nondenominational and transcendent, helping people from all religious faiths, as well as people with no religious affiliations or beliefs. As a priest, Terry ministered to youth at risk of becoming gang members as well as existing gang members in East Los Angeles at a time when that community had the highest ratio of gang-related homicides in the nation. He has served as Executive Director and Trustee of The Humanitas Prize and is a 5-time Emmy Award winner.

IMmortal Foundation helps people move from their current states to a more peaceful state of mind about life and death. Their mission resonated with me deeply. So of course I gladly took on the role of mentoring them through strategically planning their efforts to impact millions of people everywhere. Eventually I introduced them to a friend of mine who was a senior executive at a huge financial institution that loses approximately 50,000 customers each year due to death. The idea was simple:

Large companies often struggle to form and sustain meaningful connections with customers. That was certainly true for my friend's bank. Furthermore, banks are often perceived as being only about money and profit. I proposed that the bank invite all of its customers to a webinar with Lesh and Terry. Following the webinar, they could hold live events that would provide insight and comfort to customers at various bank locations and office buildings. This would involve no selling, only helping.

Real estate assets that were normally vacant in the evening would be put to good use. By holding the events at their facilities, the bankers would form stronger connections with customers than if they took place at hotels or country clubs.

Engaging customers on a topic of utmost immediate concern would not only increase connection and understanding, it could also elevate trust. When customers believe that you are truly helping them with what matters most to them, they feel understood, heard, and valued.

A partnership between IMmortal Foundation and such a bank could benefit attendees in many ways. Customers who proactively plan and prepare for death would get access to products and services before it's too late. Protecting clients from the high cost of prolonged illness or disability would build customer loyalty. Widows and widowers properly prepared would be grateful that their estate planning, long-term care insurance, and life insurance had been effectively documented and funded. Plus, surviving family members would be less likely to move their business to a competitor.

My executive friend was surprised to learn that his bank loses roughly 50,000 customers per year due to death. He also found that his company had no plans to help customers proactively and few of those customers are financially, emotionally,

> **"Try to make the world in some way better than you found it.** — *Andrew Carnegie*

or spiritually equipped to deal effectively with death. That has a far-reaching impact on family members, business partners, shareholders, and vendors connected to the deceased. A financial analysis showed that the bank would retain more customers and revenue plus create a positive impact in several of its revenue and service channels. Most importantly, they would be engaging people in ways that competitors ignore. Multiple strategic and competitive advantages were available whilst doing good in the lives of customers.

Terry and Lesh used their extensive knowledge of bankruptcy-inducing medical expenses, the fact that nearly half of America's dying can't afford their own burials, and unmet Life Insurance needs to prepare an excellent proposal for my bank executive friend. Its detail included an outline of their proposed End-of-Life Webinar that contains ground-breaking, crucial information about the personal, family, medical, legal, financial, and spiritual elements necessary for experiencing a good death.

I would like to report that the bank's joint venture with IMmortal Foundation has gone extremely well, but that isn't the case. This idea was killed in a committee before it could begin. No pilot program. Not even any meetings to explore the idea or any nuances. So tens of thousands of that bank's customers have died, less prepared and less peaceful than they could have been. Lots of long-term care insurance, disability insurance, and life insurance that should have been acquired was not. Lots of widows, widowers, and heirs who could have felt loyal and connected to the bank did not. So they moved many millions of dollars away from that bank over to competitors hoping to find more connection and proactive engagement.

Here is a simple rule to remember and thrive by:

> The one who helps most profoundly is more valued and trusted. Helping at the most crucial time with priceless wisdom and tangible solutions increases loyalty and prolongs connection. The best way to get what you want in business relationships is to help clients get what they want most in ways that transcend the imagination of clients and competitors.

My friend was shocked that his bank could not see the value and impact nor the profound competitive advantages offered on a silver platter to them via an alliance with a charity. I reminded him that people recognize value, beauty, and

Be the Client's Hero

When an opportunity to be the client's hero arises, wise professionals boldly step into that position. While all of your competitors are unable to recognize the opportunity or are unwilling to step into the role of Client Hero, you can establish yourself as being the most relevant, resonant Primary Personal Thought Leader by doing what others won't do.

Helping clients overcome their biggest and scariest challenges is the high ground that is available to you every second that you are alive. You might be able to elevate to that level on your own, but it will nearly always be easier and faster with an interdependent collaborative approach.

A partnership with the right kind of charitable organization, such as IMmortal Foundation, could speed and ease your ascension. These opportunities are available and waiting for each of us right now. The big question is: Are we willing to recognize them and seize them by acting on them before someone else beats us to that lofty position?

> **"Whoever is careless with the truth in small matters cannot be trusted with important matters.** —*Albert Einstein*

elegance to the degree they are open to and ready for it. Those who think and act interdependently with charitable intent are likely to have greater reach and impact than those individuals who act alone.

IMmortal Foundation's compassionate expertise will undoubtedly be eagerly sought after by more discerning financial institutions, but the current loss to my executive friend's bank is incalculable.

For many of us, our philanthropy is an expression of who we are spiritually. Who we donate to or provide influence for can be an exercise in self-expansion or even self-transcendence. Therefore it is not just about the money, tax deductions, or financial impact. We really owe it to ourselves to be sufficiently informed. Transparency is critical. Side-by-side analysis of advantages, disadvantages, and financial impact to all concerned is crucial if we are to optimize our philanthropic impact.

Even though most people employed by charities don't want to admit it, paid fundraisers, certain staffers, and executives are salespeople for their organizations. Many of them are insufficiently aware of the holistic full scope of complexities and viable options available to donors. They don't know what they don't know and they drive the internally created, institutionally-centered fundraising program using marketing and selling tactics much like those used by insurance, investment, and timeshare salespeople. Here is an example of what I mean:

Several years ago our firm was retained by a wealthy farming and ranching family to help them create and then implement a Macro Strategic Plan.* Part of that plan included a Net Income Charitable Remainder Unitrust (NIMCRUT) that would sell off land that had been contributed to the trust. That transaction would be tax exempt because all of it occurred while owned by the trust. During the balance of their lifetimes, Mr. and Mrs. B would receive 9% of the value of the trust as ordinary taxable income each year or what the trust earned (whichever was less). That way the trust corpus would not be invaded or subtracted from if it failed to earn 9% or more in any given year(s). There were also some income tax deductions that would benefit Mr. and Mrs. B over the next few years.

Upon the death of the second to die the charitable remainder trust corpus would be distributed by the trust to various charities including a private family foundation. Mr. and Mrs. B did not share the same religion and each of them had chosen several charities that were personally important to them to receive a share of the $5 million that was not going to their private foundation.

Somewhere in the process, Mrs. B happened to be solicited by the planned giving director of her church. Her church was promoting a variety of programs to its members. During a conversation with the planned giving director, Mrs. B mentioned that she and her husband were setting up a NIMCRUT. She informed him that she was designating one million dollars to be given to them upon the death of the last living income beneficiary either her or her husband. Not surprisingly the planned giving director immediately wanted to be involved. He offered to review all of the documents for free via the church's legal team and board of directors so that she and Mr. B could feel secure that their interests were being properly protected. After numerous conversations with this chap, Mrs. B asked me to host a meeting with all of the advisors and the charity at my office. Mr. B and I agreed to hold the meeting, but to test the sincerity and competency of the planned giving director and Mrs. B's church we did not send them any of the strategic or estate and wealth planning that had been accomplished over the past few months. We didn't send them any documents to review, which was rather upsetting to them. You must understand this important fact:

> The planned giving director and the church were certain that their one-size-fits-all program was divinely inspired and that it was so perfect that all of their members should use it without any customization at all. They also believed that their brain trust was superior to any that could be assembled by anyone else, anywhere else. Yes, they were that disconnected from reality and that arrogant.

True to form, on the day of the meeting the planned giving director and the nun in charge of fundraising sat down at our conference table and whipped out a boilerplate proposal for Mr. and Mrs. B. Then they claimed that their plan was perfect for, and in the best interest of, the B family. Neither the planned giving director nor the nun had any idea at all about what the total net worth was or what the amount of the total contribution(s) to the trust would be. They had not even asked Mrs. B to provide such data. In essence they had not offered the clients an opportunity to participate in a discovery process. Having failed to perform a reasonable level of discovery and understanding, their proposal was nothing more than a sales proposal that lacked a win-win partnership perspective.

They did what many salespeople do. They gathered some cursory information, made a long list of inaccurate assumptions, then created a perfect plan and presented it to us. Yes, they even claimed the impossible. They claimed that they were doing this in the best interest of the donor even though

> **"Men trust their ears less than their eyes.** —*Herodotus*

all of their fiduciary responsibility was with the church and therefore could not be with the B family. Needless to say, the planned giving director and the nun made no attempt to disclose the massive and multiple conflicts of interest related to their program and their advice.

Meanwhile, our firm and the lawyers and accountant engaged by the Bs were in the employ of the B's. None of us had any conflicts of interest. All of us were dedicated to and obligated to the protection and furtherance of the B's best interests. Furthermore, our extensive discovery process and full fiduciary due diligence meant that we had a well-documented understanding of the B's best interests as they were in the now, at that time. In addition, the Macro Strategic Plan® was written proof that we understood who, what, and where the Bs wanted to be next. All of that occurred prior to the creation of any trust documents, gifts, contributions, or transfers of ownership by anyone to anyone or to any trust. Our plan was extensive, completely custom, and absent any conflicts of interest.

The church's brain trust held an aggregate nationwide experience of implementing a total of 17 charitable trusts, established over the past 50 years, totaling about $4 million between all of those trusts. The team we assembled to represent the Bs had successfully implemented a few hundred charitable trusts with assets exceeding $700 million, but the story gets even better.

The proposal made by the church offered a 5% income distribution rate, which was the *minimum* rate legally permitted, and they insisted the church act as the irrevocable trustee of the trust.

When Mr. B pointed out that their customized trust could produce 9%, which was the legal *maximum* at that time, and that it had catch up provisions to make up for years when 9% wasn't earned and distributed, the planned giving director responded with a graph showing that if one or both of the Bs lived for at least another 16 years, the 5% proposed trust would begin to surpass the income of the 9% trust.

Being 70 years of age, Mrs. B said, "I'm quite sure we prefer to have the 9% trust. We might not live another 16 years." This had no impact. The nun said, "With all due respect to Mr. Wright, Mr. R your CPA, and Mr. G your lawyer, our proposal is better for you because it is God's program for you. This is what God wants you to do."

For a moment I thought Mr. B might lose his lunch. As professionals, the CPA, lawyer, and I were used to being treated dismissively or being insulted by self-serving promoters, manipulative clergy, and all manner of ill-prepared and incompetent salespeople. As real fiduciaries we were used to non-fiduciaries claiming to protect and further best interests that they had not and could not A) define in writing, nor B) actually agree to be legally accountable for.

Here is some uncomfortable truth for promoters that is good news for you as a donor or philanthropist. You get to create your very own custom program for partnering with and funding charities. You can even create your own charity that plays the role(s) you want it to play. Having your own Private Family Foundation puts you in the position of decision maker. You can succumb to the schemes of promoters or the half-baked ideas of under-informed but well-intentioned charities and their salespeople. Or you can be your own steward of your wealth. You can be a dynamic leader at a charitable organization by transcending coercion, manipulation, schemes, and half-baked good intentions. It is up to you. What type of organization you choose to lead is up to you.

If you are the top executive at a charity, will you be the leader of a charity that lives win-win with donors and their advisors? Or will your charity be like so many of the charities that take unfair advantage of naïve, underrepresented, good-hearted, overly trusting, and willing-to-help donors?

May I suggest that it is far better to form win-win, transparent constructs and relationships with everyone? Great leaders are not afraid of transparency. Great leaders want well balanced solutions that provide wins for everyone involved. Wise and effective leaders do not want to take unfair advantage of under informed people or overly trusting or gullible people. Smart leaders do not want to be tied up in court or have the reputation of their brand, company, family, or charitable organization damaged.

Informed consent requires transparency and creative and thorough comparative analysis. It also requires unusually high levels of competency and integrity. You can be the great leader of yourself and a wise steward with others. Success that endures and brings you to the end of your life with no regrets about the way you treated others and yourself is possible if you want it to be. Leaders set the tone for the amount of innovation and morality of the people around them. Yes, it's even possible to be the moral leader for those above you on the organizational chart. Organizations, families, and even societies are a reflection of the lowest moral standards that their leaders will tolerate or reward. You are hereby invited to be a morally transcendent leader who creates enduring, unregretted success.

> "Some of the best people in history do not believe in God, while some of the worst deeds were done in His name. —*Pope Francis*

Chapter Twenty-Eight

Acceleration and Elevation through Application

Reading, observing, and studying are not enough to lift you into who, what, or where you want to be next. Accurate, precise application of the right principles and actions, on time, and consistently are essential to elevation and alignment with who, what, and where you want to be next. My friend Howard Wight teaches this idea to all of his students, "Timing is *everything*, except when it isn't." Even when timing isn't urgent, doing what must be done on time and consistently enough is paramount to transcendence, innovation, and commercial or personal success. We live in complicated times when even the simplest of ideas and action plans are seldom easy to apply correctly.

Most people who read self-help books or attend related seminars and boot camps rarely elevate into a higher sense of self, significance, fulfillment, and abundance. Ascending requires more than that. It requires a combination of appropriate or relevant innovative thinking, belief, commitment, tenacity, endurance, toughness, and action(s) at the right time(s). No human is immune from any part of that recipe

When I was a boy, I often considered suicide. I even went so far as to give away my few but most precious belongings. But when the moment of truth came, I heard a quiet loving voice prompt me not to hurt myself. I was told that I was valuable and that circumstances would improve. Hang in there. Don't give up. You have marvelous gifts to share with the world.

So it's no wonder that I have a special empathy for people who are so beaten down and feeling hopeless that they are ready to give up. That's why I feel so connected to my friend Terry Kaltenbach's charitable mission.

Shortly after Terry and Linda Kaltenbach's teenage daughter committed suicide, they decided to do something to prevent this in the future. So they created their own charitable foundation called Light for Life Foundation of Southern California. Since its inception in 1997, Light for Life Foundation of Southern California has helped to enlighten and elevate an incalculable number of teenagers and others into a state of mind that stops them from ending their own lives. Elevating and enlightening people beyond the state of mind that precedes suicide is a passion for Terry and Linda. Their foundation acts interdependently with other charities, such as Yellow Ribbon Suicide Prevention Program, and donors dedicated to inspiring people to transcend depression, hopelessness, and the maladies that cause people to end their lives. For more information or to donate time, expertise, or money, please visit yellowribbonsd.org

for success today and into the future. In fact, that is also the recipe for those who want to hold on to whatever success they currently enjoy. This is why training needs to be combined with accountability either through coaching or mentoring by those who are dedicated to rising above who, what, or where they are now.

Transcendent people ascend at different paces mostly depending upon their degree of readiness to move themselves into alignment with the success or outcome they want. This entire book is about growing oneself in ways that align individuals, organizations, or societies with success, abundance, sense of significance, and tangible, measurable impact. As we grow ourselves into newer higher awareness and take appropriate precise action on time, we exercise and grow our tenacity, toughness, confidence, and courage. As we do so, we experience new and better results, greater confidence, and peace of mind about ourselves and the world around us.

I have observed that highly competent martial artists tend to be less afraid of people than many others who lack their skillsets. Preparedness and readiness in mind, body, and soul leads to greater equanimity in every aspect of life, relationships, business, and finance. Peace of mind can be grown into. We can ascend into peace of mind but we cannot descend into it. We can grow ourselves into enlightenment and highest self in life, relationships, business, finance, and government. We cannot descend our way into a consciousness or way of being that is better than where we are now.

I am concluding this book with the abbreviated stories of three exceptional women who not only thrive in business leadership positions, they also elevate everyone around them who is willing to rise.

Meet my friend and colleague, Colleen Walsh Fong. Colleen began preparing for a business career in her teens by helping her father, an executive and consultant, with administrative aspects of his business. She is an unusually smart, kind, tough, and tenacious person. Those characteristics combined with an excellent work ethic grabbed people's attention.

By the age of 28 Colleen had elevated into an executive position with a very large banking/financial institution. Back in those days, the banking profession was notorious for failing to appreciate, promote, and compensate women and minorities. In spite of that Colleen refused to be limited by prevailing business culture, small mindedness, chauvinism, and discrimination. She never thought of herself as a victim. Instead she saw opportunity and knew that she possessed the transcendent skill set to attain it. On an aesthetic level Colleen dressed the part of bank executive. She learned their language and everything essential to ascendance beyond accepted norms and expectations. More importantly, though, she delivered the substance needed to manage people and functions in a turbulent environment. Her achievements were measurable and proven.

Colleen happened to join the bank at a time when it needed significant cultural change. She applied her unusually holistic and transcendent perspectives in ways that irrefutably had a proven, positive impact on the bank's bottom line. Coworkers and those at higher levels within the organization regularly told her that problems could not be solved. But she thought beyond the status quo and developed creative ways to move the organization forward to its target. Ultimately she became known as the person to turn around areas struggling to make the necessary cultural change. It's useful to remember this:

> Organizations and individuals measure what they value, then they value what they've measured. Nearly everything else is invisible and irrelevant to them.

During her tenure with the bank, Colleen regularly received offers from consulting firms to join their teams. But she was called to entrepreneurial pursuits after she left the banking profession in 1989. Since then she has applied her transcendent abilities to monetize her talent, time, skills, gravitas, and credibility in ways that elevate her clients and the world at large. Her company, CopyWrites Freelance, produces the written materials necessary to help business leaders bridge the gap between status quo and target positions. I met Colleen when one of my business owner friends needed an excellent ghostwriter and editor. From the very beginning, she impressed me with her intelligence, equanimity, and grace. She deftly managed and led a difficult client into greater effectiveness in spite of his ego and other limiting personality quirks.

As an admirer of Colleen's articles, books, and other written materials, I had a long talk with her about this book. We explored the possibility of her taking on the position of chief editor. After reading an early and incomplete manuscript, Colleen decided to apply the principles contained herein. The resonance was amazing for her because she had already been applying many of these principles throughout her life. She achieved rapid and significant results with the teachings contained in this book because Colleen was not only ready and willing, she also applied the principles in precisely accurate ways and on time. Her implementation was consistent, even when it was uncomfortable or outside of her comfort zone. But that is what tough, tenacious, successful people do. Such people do what average people choose not to do consistently enough to succeed.

During the editing period of this book, we introduced Colleen to several of our mentoring clients who wanted to elevate as Thought Leaders and then into Market Leadership. The results have been outstanding. Our working interdependently has positively impacted our clients and it has increased the volume of people we are able to attract, engage, and elevate. Find more about Colleen, her offerings, and our joint offerings at www.TMLInstitute.com.

Recently I introduced Colleen to my colleague Yvonne Johnson. I asked Colleen to contact Yvonne to see if she would be willing to share a recent success story in this book. Fortunately for all of us, Yvonne agreed to allow Colleen to include it here.

Like Colleen, my transcendent colleague, Yvonne Johnson, owes much of her success to her habit of applying sound principles to overcome hurdles in her career. Yvonne has owned her own business, but more recently accepted a position in business development as an employee of a rapidly growing organization in the Electronic Manufacturing Services industry. Quick expansion by merger and acquisition has caused that firm to experience the usual communication and cultural difficulties that occur when different entities with different systems and cultures come together. As a business development professional, Yvonne's responsibility is to close deals that produce desired wins for clients while resulting in profit for her company. But doing that can be difficult when roles and procedures are in flux. So Yvonne has applied Transcendent Th ught and Market Leadership principles combined with those she learned from her experiences working with Japanese companies. Doing so has allowed her to stay true to her sense of integrity. Yvonne makes sure her clients improve and win from the services she provides while also ensuring that her company gains from the deals she imagines and creates.

Employees can become resistant to new ideas when they are clinging for dear life to an organization's past even when stress is due to swift growth. Finding novel or innovative ways to make services work for clients has long been a necessary component of Yvonne's success. She is excellent at that. So she works with clients to learn about where they want to be next, and helps them find, create, or buy timely impactful solutions to get there. She aligns her actions with her clients' goals. Yvonne, however, is reliant upon other executives in the organization to achieve her goals. So she lets her company's processes run as far as they can go to satisfy her clients' needs within their current structural confines. Then she becomes imaginative, innovative, proactive, and fills in the gaps with solutions she finds or creates on her own. Because Yvonne thinks like a business owner, her holistic view of both her company and her client companies cause her to understand and anticipate what both sides will need to finalize a deal. Yvonne is brilliant at bridging chasms between buyers and sellers. This empowers her to get results that ordinary executives cannot achieve.

Yvonne applies the transcendent principle of collaboration and brings all influencers and decision makers from both organizations to the table to create and agree upon final terms. Sometimes this involves multiple companies and decision makers in order to structure win-win deals. Doing so ensures that all parties agree to the responsibilities involved in providing services to the client. As a result all share in the benefits of working together. Yvonne has transcended her lack of complete authority to make all decisions, as she could do when she ran her own business, by working with co-workers in a collaborative way. She stretches herself in the opposite way of one who leaves organizational life to start her own business. She now has to think like an owner to find innovative or novel solutions for clients and think holistically for the benefit of her organization while also thinking as an employee and a coworker. She has transcended her previous orientation to excel in her new situation by applying her own truths and Transcendent Th ught and Market Leadership methods to her current professional situation.

My last example of a heroic transcendent business leader is Melinda Mordue. In my companies and those that work with them, she is known as "M." Yes, I borrowed that from the James Bond character. M leads and runs all of the daily affairs in my companies. M is a shareholder so she is tenaciously invested in our success. Many have tried to hire her away but her resonance with our purpose and the contributions we make is worth more than gold to her. M is my wife's younger sister and the only family member associated with my business ventures.

M earned her Bachelor of Science degree with a major in Psychology from Brigham Young University in 1987. Immediately after college she went to work for Novell. Not surprisingly when key executives left Novell to join Xircom, they invited and incentivized M to join them. They recognized and valued her equanimity, maturity, work ethic, and rare capabilities to get important things accomplished on time and within budget. M enjoyed working in a small but growing company. When she joined Xircom, they had less than 20 employees. She enjoyed the process of working with a group of entrepreneurs in developing programs to help a small technology company expand within the United States and then globally. She also participated in the process with them as they underwent their initial public offering. After a few years at Xircom, the company had become quite large so M decided she wanted a change from working in a big corporation. What she wanted next was to run a small but growing business. I knew M quite well and heard about the many awards she had been given from Novell and Xircom and decided to give her a chance to manage my company. Neither of us could foresee what an influential leader she would become.

Shortly after M joined my company, we created a second company to handle the Macro Strategic Planning® and business consulting we offer our professional clients. In this capacity M leads two companies and directs the administrative duties of multiple business entities as well as the individual needs within many different client projects. Together we serve consumers and business owners in helping them clearly define who, what, and where they want to be next.

Our clients appreciate the gentle yet unwavering way that M helps them accomplish what matters most to them. She embodies transcendence, being gifted at helping people identify and strengthen their talents and skill sets to accomplish goals on time and within budget. We teach and mentor professionals to increase their ability to attract exactly the types of clients and projects that fit their skill sets and bring

> **"Let those who tell you that something can't be done become your springboard to making it happen. There is always an answer. You just have to look to the world around you for the inspiration to find it.** — *Colleen Walsh Fong*

them significance and fulfillment. M works with our clients in coordinating complex schedules, preparing and processing documents, and most importantly gently encouraging and guiding them to make the shifts in behaviors that will empower them to elevate and live more majestic lives. Without her leadership, toughness, tenacity, and loving way of being, I would not be able to help as many people or transcend the challenges of business and life.

Like so many of those featured in these pages, the three powerful women described in this chapter lack the self-promotion gene. Their humility prevented them from asking me to help share their transcendent abilities and the way they act heroically on behalf of their clients or others. Humility is often a common characteristic amongst transcendent people. Part of my life's mission and my passion is to recognize the genius, heroism, and impact of transcendent people and help the world to appreciate it. I invite you to collaborate with us. You can make yourself an integral part of this vision and mission. Are you ready to come out and play big with us?

"Attitude is a little thing that makes a big difference. — *Winston Churchill*

> "My attitude is that if you push me towards something that you think is a weakness, then I will turn that perceived weakness into a strength." — *Michael Jordan*

Closing Remarks — Availability as a Catalyst

Catalyst definition: An agent, a chemical, someone or something that provokes, causes or speeds an event or change.

I invite you to consider a slight variation in definition of the word "catalyst".

Catalyst: A chemical, event, agent, person, mindset or behavior that provokes, causes, facilitates or speeds an event, epiphany or change.

Availability within our own minds, hearts and souls is a critical attribute for being tuned in so we can feel, hear, see or recognize inspiration and transcendent ideas, events, opportunities... or people. When our minds, hearts or spirits are unavailable to inspiration and transcendence, we are incapable of breaking out of our status quo or present circumstances.

Willingness and availability are like cornerstones when we want to receive inspiration or imagine, create, build or manifest any form of new outcome. Greater abundance, physical health, emotional, intellectual or spiritual strength and peace of mind are readily available to anyone who makes him or herself more available to them. Sometimes we must let go of ideas, places, things, beliefs, traditions, locations, addictions, or people that bind us to our status quo. Letting go of what separates us from availability or inspiration essential to new and better outcomes is just about as difficult or as easy as we choose for it to be.

If you keep thinking about and talking about the same ideas, courses of action and solutions, you are likely to get the same kind of results, unless your niche experiences a catastrophic "Black Swan" type of event and your existing model becomes obsolete. If your advisors continue thinking about and talking about the same ideas, courses of action, and solutions, you will continue to experience what is available within their status quo. Transcendence is always preceded by new thinking, new availability, and new courses of action. Transcendence is available to all who make themselves available to it. Transcendence is rarely available to those people who refuse to make themselves available to it. Unless you are like Jonah and God has to send a giant sea creature to swallow you so you suffer sufficiently to be willing to change and move you to where you need to be. If you want to elevate beyond your current circumstances and the status quo, begin making yourself more available to people who think and act transcendently as their way of life. Such action on your part will expose you to new ideas, new possibilities, and new courses of action that are invisible and unavailable to those immersed in the status quo. This is likely to be at least a little bit uncomfortable, but it is essential if you are to prove to yourself and to God that you are ready for and available to an elevated way of being.

This world is full to capacity with people who are playing small, who are immersed in the status quo. Many of them will live out their lives never realizing or expressing the greatness that lies dormant within them. That greatness is resting, waiting to be discovered, awakened, and expressed. It is waiting just behind the natural desire for comfort, sameness, and normalcy or the popular myths known as safety and certainty. Greatness is often waiting just beyond one's comfort, fears, addictions, favorite myths, and chosen limitations. I encourage you to rise above all that would limit you or separate you from your greatness. Step up, elevate yourself and connect with your higher self and a more abundant significant and joyful reality. Find your higher self, align with it, and make that your chosen and only way of being. Transcendent people are patiently waiting for you to begin this new adventure right now. You will find them as soon as you make yourself available to be helped by them.

A website with FREE articles, audios, videos and webinars is available to you right now. Please visit www.TMLInstitute.com. I invite you to be available to the people, the enlightenment and elevation that await you right there, right now.

Glossary

Actuate:
1. to incite or move to action; impel; motivate
2. to put into action; start a process; turn on

Ascendant:
1. a state or position of dominant power or importance
2. a position of dominance or controlling influence; possession of power, superiority or preeminence

Ascending:
1. rising or increasing to higher levels, values, or degrees
2. moving upward; rising

Audacious:
1. extremely bold or daring; confidently brave; fearless
2. extremely original; without restriction to prior ideas; highly inventive
3. lively; unrestrained; uninhibited

Balance:
1. a state in which different things occur in equal or proper amounts or have an equal or proper amount of importance
2. an aesthetically pleasing integration of elements

Dominance:
1. dominant position especially in a social, business, or political hierarchy
2. rule; control; authority; ascendancy

Elevating:
1. to lift up or make higher
2. to improve morally, intellectually, or culturally

Enduring:
1. lasting; permanent; durable
2. patient; long suffering

EQ:
1. abbreviation for emotional quotient, a.k.a. emotional intelligence quotient
2. an index of emotional intelligence

Equanimity:
1. being in the flow of knowing when to be quiet and when to speak up; when to be passive and when to be assertive
2. feeling the right timing and the right speed to create the appropriate flow
3. using reason to overcome emotional turmoil and chaos especially when others are overcome by emotion and are behaving irrationally

Ethereal:
1. extremely delicate or refined; light; airy or tenuous
2. of or relating to the regions beyond the earth

Fulfilling:
1. bringing to an end; finishing or completing
2. developing the full potential of

Holistic:
1. relating to or concerned with complete systems rather than with individual parts
2. incorporating the concept of holism in theory or practice

Impactful:
1. having or manifesting a great impact or effect
2. having a powerful effect or making a strong impression

Infinite:
1. immeasurably great; indefinitely or exceedingly great
2. extending indefinitely
3. subject to no limitation or external determination

IQ:
1. abbreviation for intelligence quotient
2. a test score commonly used to rate level of intelligence

Majestic:
1. large and impressively beautiful
2. characterized by or possessing majesty; of lofty dignity or imposing aspect; stately; grand

Market:
1. a geographic area of demand for commodities or services
2. the area of economic activity in which buyers and sellers come together and the forces of supply and demand that affect prices
3. to do things that cause people to know about and want to buy (something)

Mediocre:
1. of only ordinary or moderate quality; neither good nor bad; barely adequate
2. not satisfactory; poor; inferior

Mundane:
1. common; ordinary; banal; unimaginative
2. dull and ordinary
3. characterized by the practical, transitory, and ordinary

Need(s):
1. of necessity
2. a requirement, necessary duty, or obligation
3. urgent want, as of something requisite

Niche:
1. a distinct segment of a market
2. a place or position suitable or appropriate for a person or thing

Ordinary:
1. of no special quality or interest; commonplace; unexceptional; plain or undistinguished
2. somewhat inferior or below average; mediocre; customary; usual; normal

Pandering:
1. to tell someone what they want to hear instead of what they need to hear
2. to do or provide what someone wants or demands even though it is not proper, good, or reasonable for them
3. to provide gratification for others' desires even when such gratification is destructive rather than productive or elevating

Prostituting:
1. off ring for unworthy purposes
2. devoting to corrupt or unworthy purposes

Relevant:
1. bearing upon or connected with the matter in hand; pertinent
2. having significant and demonstrable bearing on the matter at hand
3. relating to a subject in an appropriate way

Resonant:
1. strongly affecting someone especially with a particular quality
2. intensified and enriched by or as if by resonance

Significant:
1. important; of consequence
2. large enough to be noticed or have an effect
3. having a special or hidden meaning

Similar:
1. having a likeness or resemblance, especially in a general way
2. having characteristics in common

Status Quo:
1. the existing state of affairs
2. the current situation; the way things are now

Synchronistic:
1. coincidence in time; contemporaneousness; simultaneousness
2. the simultaneous occurrence of causally unrelated events and the belief that the simultaneity has meaning beyond mere coincidence

Synergistic:
1. pertaining to, characteristic of, or resembling synergy
2. (of people, groups or companies) working together in a creative, innovative and productive manner

Transcendent:
1. beyond or above the range of normal or merely physical human experience
2. surpassing the ordinary; exceptional
3. existing apart from and not subject to the limitations of the material universe

Transformational:
1. changing in form, appearance, nature or character
2. having changed completely

Transient:
1. passing especially quickly into and out of existence
2. lasting only a short time; existing briefly; temporary

Wants(s):
1. something desired, demanded, or required
2. to desire or wish for something
3. to have a strong desire for

Whole Being:
1. a balance of Whole Brain thinking about the physical world and one's temporal self with metaphysical or spiritual perceptions, beliefs, attitudes, and behaviors
2. the combination of whole mind, whole body, heart, soul, and spirit as a way of being present in life; a soulful approach to every aspect of thinking, caring, working, giving, receiving, loving, and being alive

Whole Brain:

1. the use of one's full intellect in proper effective balance and harmony rather than relying on one's favorite or comfortable parts of the brain; balancing emotion, logic, unbiased data intake and consideration despite the discomfort associated with thinking beyond one's commonly used neuro pathways

2. disciplined extremely deep thought which pushes beyond common boundaries of bias, fear, doubt, individual beliefs, and personal desires such as safety, comfort, normalcy, certainty, and status quo

Contact the Author

To contact Bruce Raymond Wright, you may call, email, write, or connect on social media:

Bruce Raymond Wright, CEO
Macro Strategic Design, Inc.
PO Box 480
Simi Valley, CA 93062-0480
800-729-5791 or 805-527-7516
bwright@macrostrategicdesign.com

www.facebook.com/BruceRaymondWright
www.linkedin.com/in/BruceRaymondWright
www.twitter.com/ElephantGuide

Made in the USA
San Bernardino, CA
23 May 2018